Jeff Iorg has the experience... has led major change as a l... national leader, and semina... a seventy-year-old institution, he is a leader worth ...y, g.......g *Major Change in Your Ministry*, Iorg shows that trusting relationships are the key to leadership, while reminding readers that seeking God's direction should precede major changes. Leaders in churches and organizations of all sizes will benefit from this excellent book.

Thom S. Rainer
President and CEO
LifeWay Christian Resources

Every leader must continually be a catalyst for change if he or she wants to keep their organization relevant and successful. Speaking with the voice of experience, my friend, Jeff Iorg, outlines the critical components a leader must have in order to successfully navigate and guide others through this process. Every leader needs *Leading Major Change in Your Ministry*.

Kevin Ezell
President
North American Mission Board

Since 1983, I have served as senior pastor of four churches, ranging from a small church to a megachurch. In each setting I have learned the old adage is true: "Everything rises and falls on leadership." Jeff Iorg, president of Gateway Seminary, is one of the best leaders I know. He has led his organization to relocate from a dismal, stifling setting to a thriving one with unlimited potential for growth in the years ahead. In his new book, *Leading Major Change in Your Ministry*, Dr. Iorg shares proven leadership principles that have been hammered and molded in the crucible of real-life experience. I highly recommend this man and this excellent message on leadership. This is a book worth reading.

Steve Gaines, PhD
Pastor, Bellevue Baptist Church, Memphis, Tennessee
President of the Southern Baptist Convention

I've known Jeff for years, and I often talk about him behind his back—telling people he is one of the best leaders I know. Jeff has led significant changes in multiple settings, from church to academia, and he combines principles with his successful experience to help the leader understand the challenges of change.

Ed Stetzer
Billy Graham Distinguished Chair
Wheaton College

Jeff Iorg is a creative, thought-provoking, and talented writer. His books always challenge and help you at the same time. He is a leader and wants to help others be leaders too. I am grateful for his love for the Lord and the talents he has been given by God. May you be blessed as you read.

Pastor Rob Zinn
Immanuel Baptist Church
Highland, California

Dr. Iorg shares lessons he has learned in real-life ministry transitions, experienced in a variety of settings. The result is a practical book that will help any leader of any ministry anywhere. I highly recommend it!

David Johnson
Executive Director, State Missionary
Arizona Southern Baptist Convention

Honest, open, transparent, thought-provoking, clear, detailed, practical, inspiring, spiritual, forward-thinking, kingdom-driven, selfless, sacrificial, bold, persistent, God-ordained, miraculous, replicable . . . these are just a few of the attributes you will experience as you read *Leading Major Change in Your Ministry*. Most of all, the principles are proven and tested by fruit that still remains (a relocated church, a church plant that is mature, major change in a Baptist Convention, and stupendous change in one of the ten largest seminaries in the world). Thank you, Dr. Jeff Iorg, for sharing your life, and leaving key principles for kingdom advancement. With great delight, I strongly recommend this jewel to every serious leader of change. May God richly bless this work.

Pastor Brian E. Kennedy Sr.
Mr. Zion Baptist Church
Ontario, California
Preaching Professor, Gateway Seminary

Jeff Iorg uses personal experiences, biblical examples, researched facts, and common sense to lay out a clear path to pursue leadership. Jeff is a real-life leader who speaks with God-given authority. You will benefit from reading about his journey of leadership.

Jim Richards
Executive Director
Southern Baptists of Texas Convention

All of us in leadership roles know that one of our major responsibilities is leading a large group of people to undergo change. Sometimes, when the needs are great and obvious, change is easier than when the needs are great but not so obvious. Jeff's insight is so practical and helpful. I know it will enrich your decision-making and approach when you face times of leading your ministry or organization through important change.

Bryant Wright
Senior Pastor
Johnson Ferry Baptist Church
Marietta, Georgia

I have read many books on leadership, but nothing educates better than experience. Dr. Iorg takes the reader on a successful leadership journey through major change. I have found this book to be a helpful tutorial on how to provide steady, God-inspired, pastoral leadership through dramatic change—something every leader needs to know.

J. Robert White
Executive Director
Georgia Baptist Mission Board

Leading

MAJOR CHANGE

in Your Ministry

JEFF IORG

B&H
PUBLISHING GROUP

NASHVILLE, TENNESSEE

978-1-4627-7460-9

Published by B&H Publishing Group
Nashville, Tennessee

Dewey Decimal Classification: 116
Subject Heading: CHANGE \ ORGANIZATIONAL CHANGE \
MINISTRY

Cover design by Derek Thornton, FaceOut.

1 2 3 4 5 6 7 • 22 21 20 19 18

With respect and admiration, this book is dedicated to

Gary Groat, Michael Martin, Adam Groza,
Ben Skaug, Tom Hixson, and Jeff Jones

who served with excellence on the
Executive Leadership Team that created
Gateway Seminary of the Southern Baptist Convention

and to the

Faculty, staff, and families of Gateway Seminary
who sacrificed to fulfill our mission and vision.

Appreciation is also expressed to

Green Valley Baptist Church, St. Joseph, Missouri
Pathway Church, Gresham, Oregon and the
Northwest Baptist Convention

for patiently helping me learn more
about leading major change.

Contents

Prelude: A Lifetime of Leading Major Change | xi

Part One: Foundations for Leading Major Change | 1

Chapter 1: Leadership Is about Real Change | 3

Chapter 2: The Necessity of Major Change | 19

Chapter 3: When Major Change Is Needed | 35

Chapter 4: Leading People through Transition | 53

Interlude: Learning from Leading Major Change | 73

Part Two: A Model for Leading Major Change | 77

Chapter 5: Major Change Begins with Direction from God | 79

Chapter 6: Major Change Requires Initiative from a Leader | 99

Chapter 7: Major Change Is Accomplished by Followers | 117

Chapter 8: Major Change Depends on God's Intervention | 135

Chapter 9: Major Change Is Messy and Difficult | 153

Chapter 10: Major Change Glorifies God | 173

Appendices | 185

Notes | 219

A Lifetime of Leading Major Change

I *am announcing today, Golden Gate Seminary has signed an agreement to sell all seminary-owned property in Marin County."*

With those epoch-shifting words, our school embarked on an amazing journey—ultimately moving one of the ten largest seminaries in North America four hundred miles, while remaining fully operational, without significant enrollment loss or internal division.

More than just relocating the seminary—its employees, its students, and all the families involved—we created a new organizational structure (more than eighty new job descriptions), implemented a new compensation strategy, upgraded our technology infrastructure, and changed our name (with all the legal steps and branding requirements) to Gateway Seminary of the Southern Baptist Convention. As part of this, in less than three years, we built two new campuses (one in Ontario, California, and the other in Fremont, California) valued at about $60 million. In addition, we purchased and remodeled two apartment complexes for campus housing worth more than $8 million. We did all this while remaining debt free and more than doubling our endowment with the proceeds remaining from the property sale. Major change, indeed.

The Gateway Story

The relocation story really began in 2004. While interviewing for the presidency, the board informed me of the coming expiration of the master site plan (in 2009) and the need for a decision about the future status of the campus in Mill Valley (Marin County), California. For many years, people had suggested the seminary consider relocating. The board encouraged me to consider that option, as well as redevelopment possibilities, in making my recommendations to them. By 2009, we had completed extensive studies of those two primary options—redevelop the property or relocate the seminary. Our executive team recommended redeveloping the property and remaining on that site. We felt we had legal grounds to improve the campus and update the facilities for effective education in the twenty-first century. We were also concerned relocation would prove too costly—not just financially, but in our capacity to sustain operations and fulfill our mission, and in terms of the personal cost to employees and students.

When we started the redevelopment project, we selected leading professionals to guide us through the process. Our site planner had successfully managed the two largest religious/non-profit land development projects in Marin County in the past ten years. Our legal team was from the largest land use law firm in the United States. We sought counsel from and secured the support of our County Supervisor. We created a reasonable plan based on their counsel and attempted to take it through the public processes leading to adoption.

Some community groups opposed to further development in our affluent part of the San Francisco Bay Area organized to stop us. Within weeks after going public with our proposal, our County Supervisor died suddenly, leaving us without political support. We still tried various means to move the project forward from 2010 through early 2013, but to no avail. We faced entrenched opposition—large turnout at public meetings, yard signs throughout our area, picketers around our campus, neighborhood associations employing attorneys and land use professionals, and personal threats (serious enough to get a security system installed at our home). The situation was bleak. We owned a deteriorating campus in a development-averse community with the financial resources and political clout to stop us. We found ourselves less and less confident any redevelopment plan would ever be approved and more and more willing to consider other options.

Listing the property for sale, in a traditional sense, would have been counterproductive. If a "for sale" sign was erected, enrollment would dry up and new employees would be reluctant to join our team. The existing community opposition to redevelopment of the property would also discourage potential buyers. Real estate professionals advised us a traditional sale process would take at least five years. It would likely only be concluded if we were willing to enter a partnership based on the value established by the ultimate use as determined by county leaders in negotiation with our community opposition. All of these factors made a traditional listing untenable.

Early in 2013, a prospective buyer approached us. He had followed our situation and understood the development restrictions on the property. His situation was unique. He had the resources to purchase the property and personal motivations that made it an altruistic investment. For the seminary to relocate successfully, there were certain time and financial parameters that had to be met. We had three key terms for any potential sale. We wanted $100 million in cash, a two-year leaseback of our entire campus to continue operations, and an agreement with no ongoing entanglements. The buyer had to assume all future development risks.

Those terms seemed impossible to meet, and would have been for most developers. After extensive negotiations, however, we reached an agreement to sell the campus for $85 million, secured the necessary lease-back, and walked away with no further responsibility for the property. We announced the pending sale in April 2014, closed the sale in July 2014, moved the primary campus to Ontario in June 2016, and opened the new San Francisco Bay Area campus in Fremont in January 2017.

Along the way, there were multiple miracles as God orchestrated circumstances to accomplish the impossible. Those stories will be recounted in more detail later (see chapter 8). God made it clear his plan was to implement the most significant change in the history of our school. As a result, we lived and learned much about following God through major change. For me, the experience at Gateway was the latest chapter in a lifelong theme: leading major change in ministry organizations. Relocating the seminary was, in many ways, the culmination of all I had learned by leading major change in other ministry settings—experiences which proved foundational for leading the seminary successfully through its relocation, reorganization, and rebranding.

Relocating a Church

In late 1982, Green Valley Baptist Church in St. Joseph, Missouri, invited me to be their pastor. The first time we visited their facility it was apparent the church needed to relocate. They were in a small building on a gravel street less than a mile from the intersection of two four-lane arterials. The church needed to be as close to that intersection as possible, not tucked away on a back road.

The church grew during the next two years. We tried to solve space problems by starting a second morning worship service and converting old trailer houses into classrooms. This worked for a while, but none of these were permanent solutions. The only real solution—both for space issues and future strategic ministry opportunities—was relocation.

The church decided to elect a committee to search out location options in our part of town. The vote was scheduled to take place during a Wednesday night church meeting. On the previous Saturday, one of the proposed committee members stopped by a realtor's office and made a casual inquiry about available property. The realtor first thought it was for the man's business and indicated he was unaware of any suitable property. When he learned it was for our church, he changed his tune. He pulled out a drawing of a ten-acre site, platted for a subdivision, but with zoning that also permitted church use. The land was about fifty yards from the previously mentioned major intersection. He offered us the property at a discounted price—essentially his purchase price from years before plus the cost of some minor improvements. My friend brought the plans to my house that afternoon and we marveled at the offer. Within a few days the committee was elected and we told them the story of how we had learned of the available property. They were as awed as we had been when we first learned about it. After doing some due diligence on the property, we recommended the church purchase it. We had about half the purchase amount already saved for future build-ing needs and were able to raise the balance in less than a year. Today, Green Valley is a thriving church meeting in the facilities built on the new location.

Starting a Church and Building Its Campus

In 1989, God led our family to start a new church in Gresham, Oregon. Now called Pathway Church, it was formerly named Greater Gresham Baptist Church. We started with four families meeting in a public school. At its founding, the church established a conviction it would not own property or build a campus. Instead, the goal was to build a major ministry in a minor facility, growing to an attendance of one thousand and then sending two hundred people to plant another church. Pathway Church could then grow again to a thousand, and repeat the process of sending out another new church. That was the original dream that sustained us for the first ten years.

Along the way, I resigned as pastor but remained a member of the church. That's somewhat unusual, but in this case, it worked well. A few years after our new pastor arrived, God intervened to change the church's strategic direction. Through an unusual set of circumstances, God gave the church about ten acres of land in a prime location. He also worked powerfully through a capital campaign in which the church—attendance about 250—gave more than $2 million to build the campus.

When the process started unfolding, all of us were amazed how God brought everything together to accomplish this major change. The pastor invited me out to lunch and said something like this, "Jeff, I know having a building was not your dream, but it really seems God is telling us: 'It's time to build.'" I agreed enthusiastically and told him so. "I'm glad you feel that way," he responded. "Our leadership team wants you to chair the Facilities Task Force and build the new campus." I dropped my fork! "Will you pray about it?" the pastor asked. My answer was simple, "No. I'll do it. You are right. God is leading us to make this change, and if you want me to lead it, I'll do my best."

The ultimate irony was that the leader who tried to pioneer a new church model that would not require a facility was now tasked with building an entire campus. Six years and four buildings later, the campus was complete. Pathway is now one of the largest Southern Baptist churches in the Pacific Northwest, with a full program of community ministries and international missions. A major change in strategic direction and conviction about facilities helped make this possible.

Revisioning a Denomination

My reason for leaving the pastorate of Pathway Church was to become the executive director of the Northwest Baptist Convention (the regional network of Southern Baptist churches in Washington, Oregon, and northern Idaho). Making this move was a major change for me and for my family. My calling had always been to be a pastor (or so I thought), but God used an illness (cancer) to get my attention and a search committee of trusted visionaries (who could see my future more clearly than I could) to shift my ministry focus. The Northwest Baptist Convention intentionally chose me (as a younger executive director) to initiate the changes needed to capture the allegiance of a younger generation of pastoral leaders. To do that, the convention needed a major revisioning. The generation passing from leadership were the strongest proponents of this major change and were some of my strongest personal supporters. It was largely their unselfish commitment to the convention's future that made the strategic changes we implemented possible. We shifted denominational priorities to a field-based strategy designed to facilitate churches serving the world, rather than denominational staff serving the churches.

In anticipation of these changes, the convention had also decided—prior to my selection in 1995—to build a new denominational office building and training center. The groundbreaking for this new facility was held on the same day of my election as executive director. Besides implementing the major change of a new strategic vision for denominational cooperation, the second major change was building a new facility and relocating convention operations from inner-city Portland, Oregon, to suburban Vancouver, Washington. We finished that part of the project in 1997 as the Northwest Baptist Center opened. The new center housed the convention's offices and training center, the Northwest Baptist Foundation, and a regional campus of Golden Gate/Gateway Seminary.

Culmination

God has an amazing capacity to use leaders in their present situation, while at the same time using that present situation to train them for future ministry challenges. When it came time to relocate the seminary, my experience included moving an established church, relocating my family to start a church, recalibrating my expectations to include building a new church campus, and relocating staff and programs to a new denominational facility. When it came time to recast the seminary's vision, reinvent its organization, and change its name, my experience included shepherding a traditional church to step outside its comfort zone, creating a new church's organization from scratch, developing a new denominational paradigm and organizational changes to sustain it, and building facilities to house the new entity and partner organizations. My experiences were doubly useful. God had used me in each setting to accomplish his purposes while, at the same time, training me for future challenges known only to him.

Writing so much about personal experience seems awkward and might come across as self-serving. That's not my intention. My hope is these leadership experiences, along with the work done by so many colleagues in various ministry organizations, will be instructive. Paul counseled Timothy, "set an example for the believers" (1 Tim. 4:12). He also told Titus, "Make yourself an example of good works with integrity and dignity" (Titus 2:7). Peter also advocated leaders be, "examples to the flock" (1 Pet. 5:3). While leaders are encouraged to be examples, Christians are also told to imitate their leaders: "pay careful attention to those who live according to the example you have in us" (Phil. 3:17). My hope is you will find instruction and encouragement in my example—both in the failures and successes in these pages.

You will also find the perspectives of other people involved in these major changes. Key participants in each of them read the manuscript and offered helpful suggestions, bringing greater balance and clarity to the finished product. Testimonies from people who lived through these changes are also included to give voice to the followers who made them happen.

While the seminary's relocation may not be the last major change God intends me to lead, it was definitely a culmination of his purposes in my life over the past three decades. God has used me as a change agent, leading major changes in four ministry settings: relocating an established church (Missouri); starting a new church and building its campus (Oregon); revisioning a convention, including constructing new facilities (Pacific Northwest); and relocating, reorganizing, and rebranding a seminary (Gateway). These experiences have taught me the principles described in this book and illustrate these insights in practical ways.

The seminary's relocation, of course, is front-and-center throughout this book and provides wide-ranging examples of many aspects of major ministry change. While you may be in a very different ministry setting than a graduate school, the major changes experienced by the seminary will likely include aspects of whatever challenge you are facing. The seminary changed its locations, organizational structure, compensation strategies, technology infrastructure, and public identity—while simultaneously relocating or replacing its workforce and student body. Within that panorama of changes are aspects of what you are facing as you contemplate leading major change in your ministry organization.

Besides the seminary's example, various aspects of these other major changes also provide helpful illustrations of the principles outlined here. Through the experiences described in the pages ahead, I believe God will teach you how to lead the major change or changes you are facing, as well as encourage you to press forward, trusting him for success.

The first section of the book outlines foundational concepts to leading major change. The second section explains a six-fold model for leading major change. Throughout the book, the examples and illustrations are from real-life ministry challenges in both local churches and large organizations—not armchair quarterbacking. While theories about leading major change are interesting, practical insight about how to actually do it is more helpful.

The stakes are high. Leadership decisions in ministry organizations have eternal consequences. Almost every ministry organization needs—or soon will need—some form of major change. Let's get started learning how to do it.

- - - - - - - - - - - - ▶

PART ONE

Foundations for Leading Major Change

1

Leadership Is about Real Change

I f you Google "defining leadership" and click around for a while, then you will soon discover the only commonality among hundreds of competing perspectives: confusion. Leadership is described, analyzed, and lauded, but not really defined by many who write about it. When it is defined, most experts do so in their terms, based on their experiences and unique demands in their context. While nuggets of truth are sprinkled throughout these perspectives, objective insights producing a precise definition of leadership are lacking.

Judging from the confusion among students in my leadership classes, Christian leaders (and leaders-in-training) also use the word leadership without having a specific, working definition of what it means. When thirty students are asked to define the concept, thirty different definitions will be presented. These definitions have nuances spanning a wide spectrum of perspectives and practices (often based on biases emerging from limited ministry experience or proof-texting favorite Bible passages). This confusion makes it difficult to teach about leading major change because there are such widely varying understandings of what leadership really is.

Before you work your way through the rest of this chapter, try this exercise: write your definition of leadership. Craft a straightforward statement of what it means to lead. You might think, "That's easy." Try it. Write a one-sentence statement, without using any commas or conjunctions, that clearly and succinctly defines leadership. You may be surprised how hard it is to define something people talk about all the time.

This is more than a perfunctory exercise. If you are going to lead major change, you must first know what it means to lead. Once you settle on what leadership means, you will be better equipped to implement the disciplines and practices to get the job done.

An Academic Perspective

There has been a proliferation of helpful resources on leadership over the past three decades. Books by authors like Peter Drucker, Ken Blanchard, Jim Collins, John Maxwell, Patrick Lencioni, George Barna, and Thom Rainer are full of practical wisdom, catchy insights, and real-life illustrations. Books like these presume readers are more interested in learning leadership practices than analyzing leadership fundamentals or narrowly defining what it means to lead. Before constructing the superstructure, however, it is helpful to build a sturdy foundation. Developing a data-driven definition of leadership is prerequisite to knowing how to do it. Using that definition to evaluate best practices is also essential to determining the effectiveness of leadership behaviors.

At the end of the twentieth century, Joseph Rost and his research team set out to define the word leadership for the twenty-first century. Their methodological goal was formidable—reviewing every use of the word leadership published in the United States in the past century with a goal of writing a one-sentence definition of leadership. They produced a monumental study—published in an expensive, tiny-print format, mostly appreciated by other academics. This seminal book, *Leadership for the 21st Century,* provides foundational insight into the problem of defining leadership and creates frameworks for understanding best leadership practices.

A Brief History of Words

When Rost's team started scouring publications for a definition of leadership, they naturally went to the source for definitions—the dictionary. What they found reveals how recently the concept of leadership has been identified as a distinct discipline. Some of the earliest dictionaries (Candrey, 1604 and Cockeran, 1623) did not contain the words *lead* or *leadership*. By 1775, Samuel Johnson included the earliest definitions of *lead* in an English-language dictionary. He provided rather extensive definitions of *lead* but no mention of *leadership*. The earliest definition of *leadership* as "the state or condition of a leader" is found in Daniel Webster's 1828 dictionary, but is then dropped from subsequent editions (only reappearing in 1965). By 1933, the Oxford Dictionary had six pages on the definition of *lead*, but only two lines defining *leadership* as "the dignity, office, or position of a leader, esp. of a political party; also, ability to lead."[1]

Dictionary writers have struggled to define leadership, deflecting the issue by simply connecting it to *lead* and leaving it there. Contemporary sources are not much more helpful. Dictionary.com calls leadership "the position or function of a leader,"[2] and other online dictionaries mimic this tepid attempt. Defining leadership is apparently tougher than it seems.

A Brief History of Concepts

Since dictionary definitions were not that helpful to Rost's team in defining leadership, they turned their attention to discovering how the word was described, rather than defined. They worked through the literature of the twentieth century—one decade at a time—tracing the evolving uses of "lead" and "leadership." While their detailed findings are worth careful study, a summary of their insights will suffice for our purposes.

Rost's team identified six primary ways the word leadership was used in the latter part of the twentieth century.[3] These categories are still valid for describing the ways leadership is understood in the early twenty-first century. In the short summary below, one or more current examples are included as illustrations (although the output of some of these writers/teachers can fit more than one category).

Leadership as Doing The Leader's Wishes

Leadership is the leader having his or her way, getting followers to do what he or she wants, or followers fulfilling the dreams of the leader. This description descends from the "great man" theory of leadership and is exemplified in books like the popular *On Leadership* series of biographies summarizing the philosophies and practices of prominent personalities.

Leadership as Achieving Group/Organizational Goals

Leadership is the practice of facilitating groups and practicing human relations skills. This description focuses on influencing group outcomes and focuses heavily on managing people to effectively produce specific goals. Works by Ken Blanchard, international management expert, are good examples of this perspective.

Leadership as Management

Leadership is communicating the "what" and "how" of assignments and motivating followers to accomplish the tasks. This description focuses on getting people to do something and emphasizes efficient production rather than change. The leadership parables of Patrick Lencioni are entertaining examples of this perspective.

Leadership as Influence

Leadership occurs when followers comply with the leader because they want to accomplish shared goals. While coercion or force are shunned, this perspective still usually focuses on the value of healthy authoritative relationships. Books by Paul Hersey and Jim Collins are good examples.

Leadership as Traits

Leadership happens when persons with certain qualities or characteristics (natural or learned) use their gifts skillfully. The focus is on learning the trade secrets of effective leaders and shaping behavior accordingly. A very popular Christian example of this perspective is John Maxwell.

Leadership as Transformation

Leadership is a process in which leaders and followers raise one another to higher levels of motivation, accomplishment, and living. This perspective focuses on moral dimensions in both the relationship between leaders and followers and their shared activities. James McGregor Burns won a Pulitzer Prize for espousing this position in his massive work *Transformational Leadership*.

When Rost's team finished the herculean task of surveying how leadership was described in the past century, with a special emphasis on the final twenty years, they sarcastically coined this camel-like definition.[4] Leadership is "great men and women with certain preferred traits influencing followers to do what the leaders wish in order to achieve group/organizational goals that reflect excellence defined as some kind of higher-level effectiveness."[5]

While that tongue-in-check summation tried to cover every aspect of anything anyone had ever connected to leadership, Rost's team ultimately reached a more helpful conclusion. After completing their comprehensive analysis over a century of the uses of the word leadership, they offered this potent and cogent definition: "Leadership is an influence relationship among leaders and followers who intend real changes that reflect their mutual purposes."[6] That's been my working definition of leadership for more than a decade. Let's unpack it in the next section, with particular attention to how the definition begins to inform our understanding of leading major change.

The *Leading* Part of Leading Major Change

Leading major change begins with understanding what it means to exercise leadership—and that can be learned by dissecting the definition and allowing its nuances to shape leadership practices. Rost's definition has four major components. Considering them will reveal how effectively implementing each aspect is essential to leading major change.

An Influence Relationship

Many attempts to define leadership emphasize influence or some synonym that describes healthy behavioral modification or adjustment. The key to understanding how this applies to leading major change in churches and ministry organizations begins with "Christianizing" the definition.

A common critique of Rost's definition (at least by seminary students) is the failure to mention God or include any spiritual perspective. This is an important point. Rost defines leadership, not Christian leadership. Leadership is not a Christian concept, since a person does not have to be a Christian to be a leader. Rost's definition is an academic definition encompassing all kinds of leaders and leadership settings precisely because it lacks moral qualifiers. Leaders with nebulous or nefarious methods sometimes exercise influence to accomplish despicable goals. Not all leaders are Christians.

For Rost's definition to be helpful for ministry leaders, though, it must be infused with Christian meaning at key points. The first of these is shaping a distinctly Christian understanding of the phrase *influence relationship*. Ministry leaders have considerable influence because of their position, but gain significantly more influence through serving others. Jesus was crystal clear about this. He told his disciples who were squabbling over their leadership rank:

> You know that the rulers of the Gentiles lord it over them, and those in high positions act as tyrants over them. It must not be like that among you. On the contrary, whoever wants to be become great among you must be your *servant*, and whoever wants to be first among you must be your *slave*. (Matt. 20:25b–27, emphasis mine)

He later added, as if to underscore the point, "The greatest among you will be your *servant*" (Matt. 23:11, emphasis mine)/

Servant-leadership is more an attitude than an action, but it is an attitude demonstrated by actions. You cannot have one without the other. If you want to have the kind of influence required to lead major change in your ministry setting, your followers must be convinced you are passionately driven to serve them. They will be convinced by your actions, not your words. Servant-leadership is demonstrated by both professional competence and personal engagement.

One of the reasons God delayed initiating the seminary's relocation until about ten years into my presidency was to give me time to gain influence and earn trust through serving employees and students. When it came time to move the seminary, most employees were convinced they could follow me without fear they would be harmed unnecessarily by the move. Dozens of people were willing to follow (to be influenced by my decisions) because they had watched me protect people from critics, expand opportunities for service, and improve their overall compensation—for about a decade. Students had similar feelings. Although many of them had known me for less time, they were willing to follow me because of improvements over the years to seminary operations that enhanced their training opportunities. Both employees and students had also received pastoral care from me during past crises—both corporately and individually. My leadership (while sometimes self-focused and self-serving) had often benefitted others professionally (through strategic decision-making) and personally (through pastoral ministry). Those actions had convinced most of my followers they could trust me to make wise decisions on their behalf, with their overall best interests in mind.

Servant-leadership—even in large organizations—always has a personal component. Leaders who abdicate personal service opportunities are giving up a potent method for gaining trust among their followers. Some pastors, for example, have stopped making hospital visits or home visits, delegating these tasks to others or forgoing them altogether. In a large church or organization, it may be impossible to visit every hurting person, but ministering to at least some of them communicates compassion and emotional investment. In my setting, when an employee or student has a death in their family (we have about 125 employees and two thousand students), I reach out to them personally. Intentional acts of kindness when followers are emotionally vulnerable convince them you care about them, will help them as you can, and will provide the support they need to weather their storm.

When leaders serve their followers—meeting personal needs in practical ways—word gets around, your reputation for caring for followers is enhanced, and trust grows. Over the years, employees and students have often thanked me for my "personal touch." They did not expect me to meet every need. They understand time constraints, travel demands, and my daily workload prohibit me from being their personal chaplain. While meeting every need is impossible, showing concern and caring for someone in need is almost always possible. Doing this is a vital part of building the trust necessary for successfully leading major change.

Among Leaders and Followers

The next part of the definition says leadership is an influence relationship *among leaders and followers*. Leadership is a relationship between people. Like all relationships, the interaction between leaders and followers is complex, multi-dimensional, and dynamic.

Leadership relationships are complex because both parties are active in the relationship. Leadership is not something a leader does to a follower. In healthy leadership relationships, the followers are neither submissive nor subversive. They are engaged and willing to follow because they respect and trust their leader. Even in inherently authoritative leader/follower relationships (like the military), the best leaders are not those who "pull rank," but those who present a compelling mission and marshal their troops to use their insights, gifts, and talents to get the job done.

One Air Force lieutenant assumed his first command, a dysfunctional section of an aircraft maintenance building. When he arrived, he summoned the master sergeant (with almost thirty years of service) to his office. The conversation went something like this: "Sergeant, my orders are to get this maintenance section to optimal performance. You have been here a long time. What's wrong, what do we need to do to fix it, and what do you need from me to make it happen?" The sergeant replied, "Sir, with those questions, you've shown more leadership in this meeting than we've had here in a while. If you'll support me, I will get this place fixed." And, working together, they did—earning a commendation within a few months for their improvements. This young officer did not abdicate his leadership role by admitting his inexperience and asking a more experienced person for help. He clarified the mission, stated his expectations, and organized his human resources to get the job done.

Leadership relationships are non-coercive, meaning both leaders and followers have the freedom to express themselves (positively and negatively) and ultimately decide if they will remain in the relationship—either leading or being led. Leaders must always remember all followers are volunteers. That statement may not make sense at first. You may be thinking, "Employees are paid and soldiers cannot desert," but those examples do not contradict my statement.

What does it mean that all followers are volunteers? Simply, all followers decide—based on multiple factors—if they will *engage* in a leader/follower *relationship*. Many leaders have stories of disengaged employees, slacker troops, or disinterested members. These followers (in name only) were part of an organization and had no intention of leaving, but were disengaged from helping accomplish any semblance of shared mission. When leaders resort to saying, "Do it for your paycheck; do it because my rank forces you; do it because I say so; or do it out of spiritual duty," their words reveal their followers' disengagement. They have not voluntarily embraced the mission or the influence of the person who presumes to be their leader. Some of the most frustrating ministry leadership situations occur when trying to motivate persons (like callous church members) who are physically present but have no intention of participating in any shared mission. Without mutual buy-in, a leadership relationship does not exist, and real change—much less major change—cannot happen.

Leadership relationships are also dynamic, meaning they are ever-changing and ever-evolving. Leaders and followers alike are always learning new insights, adjusting to unexpected life changes, managing personal challenges, and developing new interests. The larger and more complex your church or ministry organization, the more these dynamics impact your leadership relationships. Most of us would like to assemble our team, get problems fixed, establish functional systems, and maintain the status quo (once we get things the way we like them). That is not going to happen. Once you engage in leadership relationships, you are committed to ever-changing patterns of interpersonal interaction and group interaction with your mission and its ever-evolving demands. Leadership relationships are dynamic, never static, which further complicates leading major change. Organizational change is made even harder because personal changes do not stop while corporate changes are being implemented.

Who Intend Real Change

Now we arrive at the crux of the matter. A definition, by design, is limiting. A definition both excludes and includes meaning. Our working definition of leadership includes the phrase *who intend real change.* Leadership is about change. It is about shifting paradigms, creating new approaches, and doing things that have never been done—at least not in the current setting.

Many people use the word leadership to describe all manner of organizational behavior—ascribing to persons they call leaders a wide variety of responsibilities and tasks. In keeping with the narrow definition of leadership being used here, most of what is called leadership is actually management. For some reason, the latter word puts a bad taste in the mouths of many people who prefer to be known as leaders.

Management, like leadership, is an important discipline. Good managers improve processes, create efficiency, streamline progress, and make timely decisions to keep organizations thriving. This claim may surprise you, but most "ministry leadership" is really "ministry management." For example, in a recent staff meeting with fifteen agenda items, only one called for leadership (the creation of a new academic program). The others all required management—troubleshooting problems, making incremental adjustments, allocating resources, working out misunderstandings, etc. These are managerial functions, and they are essential in every healthy organization, but according to the definition we are using, only when real change is required is leadership needed. Otherwise, managing will suffice. When major change is needed, the most skilled leadership will be required.

When a church building needs painting, that's a management decision. When a church relocates, leadership will be needed. When a church hires a new youth pastor, management is required. When a church reformats its youth ministry (like moving from a recreational model to a family-discipleship model), that's a paradigm shift requiring leadership. Good management is essential when a seminary reshapes its curriculum to improve how it trains pastors. When it starts a new program to train pastors in another culture or language, leadership will be needed.

Leadership involves real change, not incremental adjustment. Since this book is about leading major change, the next statement may be surprising. Major change does not happen very often. Most ministries need to be managed better, meaning they intentionally make incremental adjustments and gradual improvements at a measured pace. Major change makes a dramatic difference in the future of a ministry organization and usually takes time—often several years—to adequately strategize, prepare for, and implement. It is a relatively infrequent occurrence in most organizations, including most churches and ministries.

Relocating a church, building a new building, establishing a major program initiative, developing a new staffing structure, changing a church's governing procedures, starting multiple worship services or ministry sites, launching a major international mission partnership—these are examples of major changes in churches and ministry organizations. Leadership will be needed to insure changes like these are implemented successfully.

Major change, like beauty, is often in the eye of the beholder. Like describing surgery (major on me, minor on you), what seems like a small change to one person is perceived as major change to another. A pastor once called me and said, "We made a major change in our church yesterday. We moved the offering from the middle of the worship service to the end, and I think I may survive the blowback." Sadly, he was only half-joking. Some people are so entrenched, some organizations so dysfunctional, and some relationships so frayed that anything new—no matter how simple—is fraught with difficulty. Do not let these dysfunctional realities undermine your determination to lead your ministry forward. Leaders recognize when management alone is insufficient to insure future organizational health. They recognize when major change has to happen and courageously lead their followers through the process.

According to Their Mutual Purposes

The phrase *mutual purposes* is another vital place to infuse meaning into our working definition to create distinctively Christian leadership. Churches and ministry organizations have a clearly articulated mission—expanding the kingdom of God. We have different code phrases for this: fulfilling the Great Commission, making disciples of the nations, knowing God and making him known, or loving God and loving people. Specific organizations narrow these general statements to delineate their unique role. For example, a seminary trains leaders to expand God's kingdom, a mission board sends people to share the gospel with the nations, and a social service organization feeds, clothes, and cares for hurting people. These are examples of applying God's eternal mission and creating a specific, narrower organizational mission within his larger purpose.

A clearly articulated mission—both the overarching mission of God and the specific mission of a church or organization—is the key to unity between leaders and followers who intend real change. These are the *mutual purposes* to which Christians pledge themselves. Sadly, even in Christian ministries, there are self-serving people in leadership roles. There are—by biblical limitation of the concept—no self-serving Christian leaders, only self-serving people occupying leadership positions. There are also self-preserving followers—people more interested in personal comfort facilitated by organizational status quo than in accomplishing a shared mission. Fortunately, the transformation Jesus makes within believers and the Holy Spirit's impetus pushing them toward fulfilling God's mission can overwhelm selfishness and advance God's kingdom. When leaders and followers share a symbiotic relationship built around shared mission—supernatural results happen.

When the seminary's sale, relocation, and name change were announced, it was done within the context of a clearly articulated and widely embraced mission. Several years ago, through a collaborative process, we restated our mission as "shaping leaders who expand

God's kingdom around the world." By the time the major changes were announced, this mission statement had percolated through our organization for years, becoming more than faded words on dry paper. It had become part of us, our shared reason for existence, our frequently quoted purpose for sharing our work together as a seminary family. On the day the sale and relocation were announced, near the conclusion of my speech I said,

> I know your individual responses at this point are many and varied. Some of you may be too shocked to respond at all. Some may be angry—feeling like we have sold out rather than stayed here at all cost. Some may be disappointed because of your profound attachment to this location. . . . On the other hand, some of you are already dreaming about future possibilities. You can't wait to get on with the adventure. You realize this is a historic day in American Christianity. You are part of a seminary that is willing to risk everything to pursue its mission.
>
> We are walking away from a beautiful location, but we are not walking away from our mission. We are leaving behind a dilapidated campus, resource-draining political and legal turmoil, and financial demands which are getting more and more difficult to manage. But this decision is not about what we are leaving behind. It's about the future we are headed toward.
>
> Today, you are part of one of the boldest moves by any seminary in the past century. We are selling a campus, not closing our doors. We are relocating and repositioning for future success, not abandoning our vision. We are sacrificing short-term comfort for long-term fulfillment of our mission. We are positioning ourselves strategically, geographically, and financially to impact the Western United States and the world like never before.
>
> We will all pay a personal cost for fulfilling our mission and vision this way. It will, at times, be scary and unnerving.

Nevertheless, as I have told you on countless occasions, "The mission matters most." Like perhaps no seminary in recent history, we are standing behind that declaration with our actions today.

In my heart of hearts, I believe these decisions are right. I have agonized over them, and have come to believe this is God's path for us. I am going forward with every intention of finalizing the sale agreement and building a new kind of seminary for the twenty-first century.

I have made these decisions with many regrets, but ultimately, no doubts. We are headed to the future, and I hope you will join me on the journey.

The mission matters most is more than a catchphrase at Gateway Seminary. Those words have come to define our mutual purpose—a purpose for which we have sacrificed much. The unity we demonstrated through the multi-year relocation process resulted primarily from hundreds of people rallying to the mission. When people passionately devote themselves to mutual purposes, amazing progress is possible because supernatural results occur. God camps around people who embrace his mission and share his mission with each other. His presence was palpable as we went through the journey together.

As an alumni and faculty member of Golden Gate/Gateway it was hard to imagine letting go of our Mill Valley Campus. Over many decades it was a formative place that trained thousands of ministry leaders for a lifetime of service and devotion to God. Although the obstacles were clear and God's provision was certain, there was still a deep sense of loss in preparing to leave such a meaningful place. Yet, in the midst of this, many recognized the importance of taking this step of faith so the seminary could continue to impact lostness in the years to come.

During the final year in Mill Valley, we had several events to engage alumni in the transition process. Many prayer-walked the campus, took pictures in front of "the bench" (overlooking the bay), or met up with old friends at special gatherings. Those moments provided opportunities to reflect on God's goodness in the past and his continued faithfulness to carry us forward. Gateway's legacy through Golden Gate Seminary was not forged around buildings or a beautiful view, but around a continued commitment to work together to shape leaders who expand God's kingdom around the world. One alumnus, Tim Howe, said it best when he concluded, "The sending place has become the sent one."

Lisa Hoff

Another Foundational Issue

Leadership, by definition, is about change—sometimes major change. Some leaders, and even more followers, are reluctant to initiate major change. They just do not want to rock the boat. They may be annoyed by nagging problems in their church, in denial about the slow death their ministry organization is experiencing, or reluctant to forsake personal privileges to accomplish a mission larger than themselves. No matter the reason, they are unwilling to move forward, preferring present problems to future possibilities. Some justify their spiritual inertia by claiming real spiritual leaders protect people and avoid creating organizational upheaval or personal pain. They may even quote verses about loving others or peacemaking for scriptural support of their commitment to the status quo.

Is major change sometimes necessary, even when it's disruptive? Are leaders responsible to initiate change when they know it will inflict pain on their followers? Should leaders ask for or even demand sacrifice from followers to fulfill God's mission through their church or ministry organization? These are fair questions. Let's discover what Jesus had to say about these issues as we move on to consider the necessity of major change.

2

The Necessity of Major Change

L eading major change is disruptive and can be messy and difficult for both leaders and followers (see chapter 9). When leaders initiate major change, they upset organizational equilibrium, create uncertainty for people, likely cause personal challenges, and usually call for sacrifices of time and money. A sobering and legitimate question is, given the turmoil that often results, "Should Christian leaders initiate major change?" Given the subject of this book, the answer may be obvious, but it is often *painfully* obvious for leaders and followers. That is the part of major change that causes many leaders to make peace with their status quo rather than forge ahead to God's future for their ministry organization.

Creating Chaos

When grappling with the dilemmas about relocating the seminary, the most troubling aspects were the significant personal challenges the decision would create for employees and students. Outsiders presumed the greatest relocation challenges were keeping the seminary operational and making it stronger for the future. They also marveled at what would be required to pack and move an entire seminary, build two new campuses, create a new organizational plan, and hire dozens of people to staff it. But those were not the issues that kept me up nights worrying through the decision.

Solving organizational challenges was not the most difficult part of the relocation. We had a high-quality management team capable of handling those issues, and our shared commitment to our mission sustained organizational functions. Once our constituents had the facts, we felt most of them would agree the decision was best for the seminary—organizationally, strategically, educationally, and financially. The greatest stressor was dreading the personal impact the decision would have on employees, students, and their families. The ominous, oppressive weight of anticipating the chaos this decision would create in many lives made for many long nights. Most Christian leaders are pastors at heart—no matter our leadership role, title, or office. We want to solve problems for people, not cause them. The decision to relocate the seminary was made more complicated by the turmoil it would create for dozens of families.

One employee had a teenage daughter in an educational program perfectly suited to her unique needs. They had worked for years to get this program in place—coordinating the teaching plans, class schedules, and even complex transportation issues. This young woman was thriving and we were all proud of her and happy for her family. Moving the seminary ended this educational opportunity.

One grandmother had all her grandchildren within a short drive of her home. She was happy and content. God had given her husband a ministry he enjoyed, while at the same time providing good jobs for her two sons in close proximity to the seminary. This extended family served in a church together and was a model of Christian interaction and multi-generational family dynamics. The relocation fractured their idyllic world.

An employee's wife had a lucrative position in the medical field. She had been promoted to a significant responsibility where she helped save lives. Over the years, her income had increased substantially—due both to the affluent area where the seminary was located and her competence. She gave it all up when the seminary moved.

One employee had been with the seminary for more than twenty years. He was not quite old enough to retire but felt too old to start over in another location. He did not have a large extended family, but his friends were all in the Bay Area. We asked him to relocate and offered him inducements to do so, but he decided to end his employment and face the challenges of starting a new job later in life.

When the president announced the seminary was moving, we knew major changes were coming—but the ball was not in our court. As a full-time pastor and a half-time faculty member, I knew I could not move to Ontario as a part-time employee with the seminary. It just was not financially feasible.

Two weeks after the announcement, seminary leaders invited me to move south and become a full-time faculty member. The dilemma of leaving a twelve-year pastoral position in a Bay Area church meant our family spent the next several months praying. We understood the Lord was opening a door for what might be our final chapter of full-time ministry before retirement. We also knew, after forty-four years in ministry counseling others about these issues, that leaving a healthy church situation was one of the hardest decisions ministers make. This would prove true for our family as we struggled with the tensions between needs in the Bay Area, the stability we had in ministry, and accepting the new opportunity with Gateway.

Glenn Prescott

Besides these employees, the relocation decision also impacted students. Many decided to accelerate their programs to graduate before the seminary moved (which meant finding additional tuition money and more time in already busy schedules). Other students had to revise their educational plans, taking more online courses or switching to a different campus to continue their training. While we had good processes in place to manage these issues, we could not eliminate the personal chaos the relocation forced on students.

Many employees and students also served churches, which meant decisions had to be made about future leadership commitments and roles. Just like employees, students also had spouses with jobs, children in school, and health concerns with established treatment programs. The average age of seminary students today is mid-thirties. They are not kids; they have kids! When we were considering the relocation, we knew the fallout among student families would be significant.

We also knew, in a more indirect way, the relocation and resulting name change would impact our nearly nine thousand graduates. They proudly graduated from Golden Gate Seminary. Like all schools, we have shared memories and a spiritual heritage—much of it tied to our former campus overlooking the San Francisco Bay. People met their spouses, got engaged, had children, and answered God's call to their first ministry assignment on what was, for thousands of people, "holy ground." This sacred space was consecrated by their life-changing encounters with God during their student years. Many graduates have children who had come to Golden Gate as students, some even living in the same apartment their parents had used many years before. Selling the campus felt like we were selling the communal heritage of the Golden Gate family. Our collective memories were at risk when we closed those doors the final time.

Inflicting Pain

Several years ago, a trusted friend told me, "You can't lead if you can't inflict pain." That struck me as wrong on several levels, and for some time I tried to disprove what became prophetic words. Christian leaders are supposed to do good, make life better, and find ways to alleviate stress and conflict—not cause it. But the longer I considered his observation, in light of both biblical examples and personal experiences, the more accurate and applicable it became.

Leaders intend real change—and that is often painful. It causes organizational upheaval and personal angst. Leaders' decisions sometimes inflict pain on their followers. Good leaders do not enjoy hurting others, but are responsible to make difficult decisions (in the short run) for the long-term benefit of advancing God's mission and the particular mission of the organization they lead.

These observations raise the question—a seminal question for Christian leaders when it comes to making pain-inducing leadership decisions: *Does God want us to do this?* Does God—who loves both leaders and followers—ever want a leader to initiate major changes, knowing they will produce painful consequences for everyone involved?

The answer is clearly "yes." The Bible has many examples of God instructing leaders to take people into battle (both physical and spiritual), take positions that divided communities, or risk life-threatening situations as part of accomplishing his greater good.

Physicians take an oath to "do no harm." They understand causing pain, like when setting a broken bone, is different than doing harm. They often cause short-term pain for long-term gain. When a limb is set properly and heals completely, the painful treatment is remembered as a necessary step in the healing process. The ultimate good makes the temporary bad acceptable. Christian leaders inflict pain, but try to avoid doing any harm in the process.

Jesus made some of his most pointed statements about the need for change—including the need for major change. He did so using illustrations that pictured the far-reaching implications and challenges of making those changes. Before considering those illustrations, let's take a look at the context in which those principles were first shared. Jesus taught about the necessity of major change while dealing with people experiencing dramatic change and struggling with its implications and personal costs.

Responding to Major Change

Matthew 9:9–15 records three encounters Jesus had with people experiencing the biggest change of all—the inauguration of his kingdom.

> As Jesus went on from there, He saw a man named Matthew sitting at the toll booth, and He said to him, "Follow me," and he got up and followed him. While he was reclining at the table in the house, many tax collectors and sinners came to eat with Jesus and his disciples. When the Pharisees saw this, they asked his disciples, "Why does your teacher eat with tax collectors and sinners?" Now when he heard this, he said, "It is not those who are well who need a doctor, but those who are sick. Go and learn what this means: I desire mercy and not sacrifice. For I didn't come to call the righteous, but sinners." Then John's disciples came to him, saying, "Why do we and the Pharisees fast often, but your disciples do not fast?" Jesus said to them, "Can the wedding guests be sad while the groom is with them? The time will come when the groom will be taken away from them, and then they will fast."

Jesus met Matthew at his tax collection booth, the Pharisees at a dinner party, and John's disciples soon thereafter. Each of these represents a typical response to major change.

The Matthew Model

The first person Jesus encountered in this three-story progression was Matthew. Jesus may have had a prior relationship with Matthew, but the brevity of their recorded interaction communicates how definitive this moment was for Matthew. Jesus met him at his place of business, a tax collection booth, and invited him to become his follower. His invitation was simple and direct, "Follow me." Without fanfare, the Bible reports Matthew's acquiescence and obedience. Since Matthew later wrote this Gospel, it's interesting he did not record any additional dialogue or his inner thoughts about this life-changing moment. Jesus called. Matthew answered. Case closed.

But, in its context, there's much more to the story. Matthew was a tax collector, a collaborator despised by the Jews (for selling them out) and the Romans (for being unprincipled and able to be bought). First-century tax collection was a racket, rampant with abuse. It is hard to imagine a more despised profession from which Jesus would call one of his most prominent followers (Matthew's stature is confirmed by his writing a Gospel). The absence of any commentary by Matthew, even with time to reflect before telling the story, is striking. Since Scripture's production was inspired by the Holy Spirit, this story was recorded precisely this way to make a point. Jesus calls people who become his valued followers through simple obedience. The kingdom of God was dawning, made up of people like Matthew who most religious leaders of their time considered embarrassing socially, inferior culturally, and anathema spiritually. This was a major change for everyone.

The Matthew model of change is clear: hear Jesus and follow him. That seems simple, and in some ways it is. The decision to participate in a major change can be boiled down to this formula: hear Jesus and follow him. He is still directing people today, and our task, more than ever, is hearing from Jesus and getting in step with his instructions. While discerning Jesus' direction is often challenging, doing so is fundamental to the change process. As part of the model for leading major change, we will consider how leaders and followers discern God's direction today (see chapter 7). For now, just remember this foundational principle: hear Jesus and follow him when it comes to making major change.

The Jesus/Matthew interchange and how it was recorded sets up the next two stories. Matthew was a known sinner. The next two groups represent entirely different people with very different problems with the changes Jesus was introducing.

The Pharisees' Problem

The Pharisees were the religious elites of their era. As part of their legalistic leadership, they created an elaborate system of ceremonial hand washing, complete with rules about what to eat, with whom to eat, and how to eat without being contaminated. Those rules had been centuries in the making. Jesus obliterated them at one dinner party.

After securing Matthew's commitment, Jesus attended a gathering at his house. The other guests were Matthew's friends, whom he later described as "tax collectors and sinners" when he wrote the story. Jesus reclined at table with them, shared food with them, and maybe even touched them. Scandalous!

The Pharisees saw this brazen disregard for their food consumption and hand washing standards. They were aghast. They could not believe any rabbi would stoop so low. Being seen in the presence of wicked people was bad enough, but Jesus was eating with them—sharing table fellowship with unwashed masses. The Pharisees confronted Jesus' disciples with this pointed question: "Why does your Teacher eat with tax collectors and sinners?"

The context of these events is significant. This story stands in contrast to Matthew's response to Jesus just described. It is also a prelude to Jesus' teaching about major change coming in just a few verses. With that in mind, what does the Pharisees' question reveal about their problem with the kingdom of God dawning in their midst? The Pharisees were upset too much was changing too fast. They and their forefathers had spent millennia creating and perfecting a religious system that kept them in power and everyday people in bondage. They were not about to let it all slip away because one rogue rabbi was flouting their religious traditions.

The Pharisees represent people so wedded to their religious systems that they fossilize practices, preventing change from ever occurring. In the process, they diminish their relationship with God and grow to resent those who create new methods for people to find their way to

God. They are obstructionists who complain about change and defend the status quo, often in the name of God. That is the worst part of dealing with these people. They really believe God is on their side, and anything that contradicts or countermands their position cannot be from God.

When we relocated the church in Missouri, one person opposed the move with pharisaical precision. He told me, "God gave us this church building. If he didn't want us to have it, he would not have given it to us. God wants us here." Many people use similar reasoning to oppose other changes. Like the Pharisees, they are convinced God "got it right the first time" and no change is needed—not in Bible translations, worship styles, church locations, seminary curriculum, missionary strategies, or anything else that is just the way they like it.

When it comes to major change, we must avoid the mistake the Pharisees made. They took positive aspects of God's revelation—the food and cleansing laws in the Old Testament—and turned them into legalistic rituals that became their god. Idolatry was their sin. When we resist change by ascribing eternal permanence to human-created systems or methods, we do the same thing. We become idolaters, more committed to preserving religious practices than practicing a living faith in an active God.

The Pharisees felt the pain of losing power and forfeiting prestige. They may have also feared financial loss and losing face with secular authorities who depended on them (and colluded with them) to control what was often perceived as the Jewish rabble. Major change caused them personal, professional, and political pain that they were determined to avoid. While we judge them harshly in hindsight, the sobering reality is we can drift into this perspective without spiritual diligence. Any time we cling blindly to historic systems rather than respond to God's present-day activity, we become Pharisees in our perspective on change.

John's Disciples' Problem

Soon after the Pharisees' concern was answered, a second religious group came forward with another question revealing resistance to change. John's disciples asked, "Why do we and the Pharisees fast often, but Your disciples do not fast?"

John's disciples were classic early adopters.[7] They had responded positively to the preaching of John the Baptist, repenting of their sin and embracing his vision of a coming Messiah. As they were meeting Jesus, they were gradually transferring allegiance to him. Keep in mind the limitations of first-century communication systems. They were much slower than today, depending on word-of-mouth communication and tedious transportation methods. No one sent a mass email or hopped on a plane to tell John's disciples to start following Jesus. Their transition was a process. They kept following John's ascetic practices (like fasting) while learning what it meant to follow Jesus.

As early adopters, John's disciples saw change coming and embraced it. When they heard John's preaching and saw his separated lifestyle, they turned from their past way of life and adopted outward demonstrations of their earnest spiritual devotion. John lived in the desert and ate honey and wild locusts. His followers were certainly willing to deny themselves and demonstrated their devotion by fasting.

This was the background to the question John's disciples asked Jesus—"Why do we and the Pharisees fast often, but Your disciples do not fast?" In the context of this section of Scripture on change, what were they really asking? The disciples of John were saying, in essence, "Jesus, we fast and the Pharisees fast, but your disciples do not. What gives? You need to tell your guys to get with the program. They need to pick up their spiritual pace. It's time to get serious!" John's disciples had embraced major change and wanted others to change faster. Their problem: things were not changing fast enough.

The Pharisees were legalistic traditionalists, laggards who exemplified both active and passive resistance to change. John's disciples

illustrate the opposite problem. They were early adopters who com-
plained others were not changing fast enough. Like the Pharisees, they
claimed a spiritual motivation. God—through John's preaching—had
asked them to change. They had done so, and were openly demonstrating their devotion through fasting. Now it was time for everyone else
to stop dawdling and make the same changes. John's disciples represent
people who are frustrated with leaders who are moving too slowly.

Jesus' answer helps leaders today understand how to deal with impatient followers. Jesus used an illustration of a wedding celebration—not
the time or place for fasting—to make this point: there is a time and
place for everything. Jesus did not rebuke John's disciples for their zeal or
express frustration with their question. He answered with an illustration
to help them understand the pace of change is often as important in determining success as the nature of the change itself (see chapters 3 and 5).

Coming into my new role as a denominational leader in the
Northwest, I anticipated the most frustrated people would be those
who thought my pace of change was too slow. Since I was coming from
the pastorate of an innovative church, had a reputation for embracing
change, and was given a mandate from the board to make significant
changes, many assumed the changes would come fast and furiously.
They did not. We made major changes, but they were done in a measured way through established procedures and protocols. As predicted,
the most frustrated leaders were not the old warhorses who appreciated
the pace of change (and ultimately embraced the results). The most
impatient were the young broncos chomping at the bit for changes
reflecting their culture and generation. While it was at times a tenuous
dance, keeping a steady pace with the major changes we enacted helped
both groups find common ground and work together.

Diagnosing Responses to Change

Jesus interfaced with three unique situations, each illustrating
a perspective on how people respond to major change. Some people

(like Matthew) make an ideal response—they hear instructions from God and move forward obediently. After leading others for about forty years, this response seems like more of an elusive ideal than a frequent reality. On my best days, this pattern prevails: I hear God's instructions (through his Word and the Holy Spirit's promptings) and obey him. Unfortunately, my inconsistency and spiritual dullness limit the frequency of my "best days" when that happens. Depending on the issue, I careen between the two extremes modeled by the Pharisees and John's disciples. I am frustrated too much is changing too fast or not enough is changing fast enough. Most of my followers have these same experiences.

You may disagree, claiming, "I like change. I am always open to new ideas and embrace them readily." Most people who make this claim really mean, "I embrace change when the change is something I think needs to be changed." In reality, all people—including leaders—struggle to live out the Matthew model while battling with the issues raised by the other two groups Jesus encountered.

For example, the American League adopted the designated hitter rule in 1973, forever compromising the historic perfection of baseball as it was meant to be played. That was an unnecessary change—a blight on the game for more than four decades. A good friend, baseball fan, and sometimes teaching partner in a seminar on change always interrupts my lecture at this point and shouts, "Best decision ever." Point made. On many changes, differences of opinion lead to different perspectives on the relative merit of the change. Some people see it one way; others see it quite differently.

Leaders who initiate major change must remember people respond to change in a variety of ways. While the people Jesus encountered illustrate three categories of response, they are not rigid silos. There are subtle layers or shades of response within each of these categories and the categories can blend together or overlap. Recognizing people respond to change in a myriad of ways and diagnosing how to lead them through major change requires discernment and determination. In the next two chapters, we will learn two more foundational insights about how people process change and move through transition. But before we do, let's consider two significant principles Jesus taught underscoring the necessity of major change.

Jesus Calls for Major Change

Jesus used two illustrations to teach about the necessity of major change. These examples were based on common experiences of his hearers (which need some explaining to make sense to a modern audience). These stories teach timeless principles about change and provide baseline insights into leading major change successfully.

No Patches

Jesus taught the first principle about the necessity of major change with a sewing illustration. He said, "No one patches an old garment with unshrunk cloth, because the patch pulls away from the garment and makes the tear worse" (Matt. 9:16). In the first century, when a child needed a new shirt, the first step was shearing a sheep. The shorn wool was then spun into thread, woven into cloth, cut into pieces, and sewn into a suitable form. After the child wore the garment a few times, it would be soiled. The shirt would then be removed, washed in a river, pounded clean on a rock, and hung up to dry. Each time this was done, the garment would shrink and change shapes. Eventually, it would tear and need to be repaired.

Jesus stated the obvious—at least to everyone who heard him that day. An old garment cannot be restored by sewing on a patch of new cloth. If you do that, when the cleansing cycle is repeated, the new patch will shrink differently from the old garment, making the tear even worse.

The illustration teaches this principle related to major change: patches do not work. A patch is insufficient to solve an entrenched problem. Gradual change is often desirable for lesser concerns. Minor problems can be solved with course corrections. Good management (see chapter 1) resolves many issues. Big problems, however, require major changes. In those cases, a patch is not sufficient.

Some changes cannot be made incrementally. For example, suppose your state decided to switch the side of road where cars are driven—from the right to the left. Would you want that phased in gradually, county by county? No way! Changes like this are all-or-nothing, paradigm-shifting, no-going back breakthroughs. Everyone has to make the change at once—no exceptions, no outliers, and no recalcitrant naysayers who insist on the old ways. When God directs his people to make a major change, he means *make a major change.* No patches!

New Wineskins

Jesus taught a second principle about the necessity of major change with another illustration from daily life in the first century—the use of wineskins. He said, "And no one puts new wine into old wineskins. Otherwise, the skins burst, the wine spills out, and the skins are ruined. No, but they put new wine into fresh wineskins, and both are preserved" (Matt. 9:17). In Jesus' time, wine was often fermented in wineskins. A wineskin was a pouch formed from a fresh animal hide, stitched together to form a pliable container. Grape juice was poured into the wineskin, and it was capped and hung up to age. As fermentation happened, the wineskins expanded to contain the wine being produced. New wine (fresh juice) required new wineskins so the container could expand as the juice fermented.

In contrast, new wine could not be put into old wineskins. No person would retrieve a battered, brittle wineskin and reuse it after it had lost its elasticity. Putting fresh juice in that container would prove catastrophic. As fermentation occurred, the wineskin would crack—even rupture—and the wine would be lost. Jesus then restated the obvious: new wine goes in new wineskins.

The illustration teaches a second principle related to major change: new structures are necessary to sustain change. Making major change requires new structures (new budgets, new organizational charts, new buildings, new policy manuals, etc.) to hold and support the change. This is often the hardest part of making a major change. Leaders often announce the change, but fail to create the organizational structures to reinforce it. Followers may claim to embrace a major change, but then sabotage it by resisting the necessary steps to fulfill its implementation. Whether leaders fail to create a new wineskin or followers refuse to embrace it, the results are the same. No new wineskins means no sustainable changes.

When we relocated the seminary, we made several strategic changes to our organization, including new positions, new supervisory structures, new job descriptions, new performance expectations, and a new compensation strategy. We made sure all five of those changes were congruent with each other and supported the new organization we were creating. We were successful in creating a new organization because we created a five-fold "new wineskin" to support, hold, and shape the changes being implemented. Trying to force new outcomes from old organizational wineskins would have been counterproductive. Major change *requires new structures to be successful.*

Diagnostic Tools Are Needed

Making major changes in churches and ministry organizations can be painful and chaotic. Still, wise leaders know they must hear God's direction and lead their followers to obey him. When we are at our best, we do it as simply and definitively as Matthew. Mostly, however, we (and our followers) are more like the Pharisees and John's disciples. We carom between the extremes of resenting too much change or complaining not enough is changing fast enough.

Most changes in ministry organizations are incremental—more managerial adjustments than real paradigm shifts. Sometimes though, when it is time for a breakthrough, major change (and all that goes with it) is necessary. Major change means patches are not sufficient and new structures are required. Jesus taught those important principles to motivate and instruct us about leading change.

Since leading major change is a biblical mandate, how do you know when your organization needs to make a major change? When is major change an organizational necessity? Determining if and when to initiate a major change is a crucial challenge for leaders in any ministry. In the next chapter, we will move beyond intuitive guesswork about the options and discover diagnostic tools to guide in answering these questions.

3

When Major Change Is Needed

Deciding when major change is needed is a weighty responsibility. It is one of those "the-buck-stops-here" aspects of leadership. Since major change impacts the mission, vision, values, and long-term viability of a church or ministry organization, a senior leader cannot abdicate or delegate this responsibility. These decisions have the most far-reaching impact on current constituents as well as future effectiveness. In addition, they have eternal consequences for people depending on ministries to spread the gospel and facilitate disciple-making and Christian service. For all these reasons, decisions about major change require thoughtful, prayerful, courageous leadership.

Leaders need more than an intuitive feeling, an experienced hunch, or a moving emotional moment to solidify a decision to lead a major change. Using a series of diagnostic questions to guide this kind of strategic decision-making helps clarify the issues and produces a more measured, data-driven conclusion. Asking these questions in the context of submissive prayer before God and collegial humility among your leadership team makes answering them a spiritual quest, a path to discovering God's direction. The key diagnostic questions are:

1. Is the change essential to the mission?
2. Is there shared urgency about the change?
3. Is relational trust high enough to sustain the change?
4. Is the timing right for the change?
5. Am I willing to see the change to completion?

The issues raised by these questions—essentiality, urgency, trust, timing, and completion—must be probed honestly and thoroughly. Nuances and implications must be carefully considered, with dogged determination to find the best answers. The stakes are high as you answer these questions. The future of your ministry may be in the balance—and that is a sobering reality for leaders who care more about advancing God's kingdom than anything else.

Essentiality

The first diagnostic question—"Is the change essential to the mission?"—is intentionally listed first. It is the most important question because it gets to the heart of the reason for major change. It is easy to be confused and forget the only legitimate reason for leading major change—advancing the mission of your ministry organization as it serves God's mission.

There are at least three problems clouding the issue when answering this question. First, leaders can initiate major change to meet their ego needs (all the while using "mission language" or "God talk" to validate their decision). For example, a pastor may want the accolades given to large church pastors, so he insists on erecting a worship center his church cannot afford—all in the name of evangelism and missions. In some cases, a new building may be essential to reaching more people with the gospel. But when the project straps people financially with unreasonable debt or depends on the preaching gifts of one person, the facility serves ego more than mission. The decision may be described in high-sounding spiritual verbiage, but it is really about satisfying the leader's needs.

In my first pastorate, when our attendance was still less than two hundred, I decided we needed a television program on a local public access channel. I envisioned a talk show/Bible teaching format, with me hosting interesting interviews followed by a riveting Bible message (by yours truly, of course). We spent months working on this project, the church spurred on by my insistence this was a forward-thinking strategy for reaching more people with the gospel. Finally, good sense won out of over youthful ego. We pulled the plug on a project that was dead on arrival, only driven forward by my out-of-control ego. Ouch!

A second issue about the priority of mission in major change is initiating it to make people (leaders and/or followers) more comfortable. Most legitimate major change does the opposite. Still, it is tempting to increase compensation, streamline organizational practices, or even add staff members to care for constituents rather than fulfill the ministry's mission. These decisions are often popular and earn kudos from followers, making them more appealing than decisions that produce major change aligned with God's mission.

One pastor wanted his church to add an associate pastor to alleviate some of his workload. He did not understand adding staff increases workload for supervisors, not lessens it. He was challenged to think about hiring someone who could train more lay leaders (thus advancing their mission)—not just pick up the slack on onerous tasks he did not want to do. The major change he wanted was about his comfort, not his church's mission.

Finally, another problem related to prioritizing mission when deciding about major change is making changes that actually serve the organization's mission—but without improvement commensurate with the expense and effort it takes to accomplish the changes. Although we moved the seminary, we always had the option of remaining in our former location. We could have stayed and continued to fulfill our mission in ever-diminishing ways as more and more resources were diverted to maintaining a legacy property. Redevelopment (just like relocation) would have been a major change, just not one that would have produced enough mission advancement to justify the cost—human or financial.

Major change must be made for one reason—advancing your ministry's mission as it aligns with God's mission. Some might bristle at the emphasis on organizational mission instead of purely advancing the mission of God. Advocating advancing the mission of your church or ministry rests on the assumption its mission is within the larger mission of God. If not, aligning your organization's mission with God's mission is a step you must take before initiating any other major change. Stop reading and get that fixed before attempting anything else.

While living on the Mill Valley campus as a student, I experienced many wonderful moments—like the birth of our oldest daughter and graduating as part of the fiftieth anniversary class in 1994. I loved that place—foggy mornings, amazing views, and spiritual memories. Seventeen years later, my service as a trustee began with learning about the development challenges we were facing.

The community and political leaders had a political stranglehold on the seminary's development process. It was maddening. A nightmare. When all the facts were known to the board, the choice to sell the campus and move was not a choice at all. There was no way God wanted to put the seminary's mission on hold for ten years to sue the county, fight in courts, and spend millions of dollars to win a legal battle simply to renovate and expand a campus. We prayed. We prayed some more. And we waited.

Amazingly, the Lord brought us a buyer. Hallelujah! But it was hard, too. Our beautiful campus associated with so many memories would be sold by my vote. I was excited and sad. The Lord reminded me again and again his mission of lives being saved for eternity is far greater than any grassy campus with a panoramic view. He was going to use the campus in a beautiful way to accomplish his mission—just not in a way any of us imagined a few years before. What an honor to be part of making that decision.

Jeff Evans

Every church or ministry organization needs a short, one-sentence mission statement (written without commas or conjunctions) that succinctly declares its reason for existence. For example, our mission at Gateway Seminary is *shaping leaders who expand God's kingdom around the world.* We adopted that statement several years ago and use it frequently in organizational planning. When we were deciding whether to continue our development battle or initiate the relocation, our leadership team often debated which decision would best fulfill our mission (not which decision was easier, more comfortable, or less costly).

Over the years, an additional phrase had become important to our seminary community—*the mission matters most.* We often challenged our students to remember that slogan as they graduated and moved into ministry leadership. As our executive team and board discussed the development/relocation options, we challenged ourselves with the same phrase—*the mission matters most.*

Several years into the land development versus land sale process, we came to a crossroads when a sale/no sale decision had to be made. Our executive team experienced a pivotal moment, centered on our continued emphasis on fulfilling our mission as the reason for major change. Michael Martin, vice president for academic services and longest serving seminary employee (more than thirty years), was thoroughly involved in the decision-making process and, like the entire team, agonized over the options. Mike is an earnest Christian, careful academician, process-oriented decision-maker, and is passionately committed to our school. Golden Gate/Gateway has been his life's work. To say he is invested is a huge understatement.

In a particularly crucial meeting, I said, "We have to decide if selling the property is the best way to fulfill our mission. Our mission is shaping leaders. Our mission isn't winning land development conflicts, reforming dysfunctional planning commission processes, or beating our neighbors in legal battles. Our mission is shaping leaders." Mike then added, speaking softly but directly, "Jeff, holding onto historic property and preserving institutional legacy are also not our mission. Even if we close the seminary, if more leaders are trained and God's kingdom advances as a result, we will have done the right thing." And then Mike said these sobering words, a conclusion he voiced aloud for the first time which helped shape our destiny, "Jeff, we have to sell the property."

In that moment, although we were some time away from the final decision, it was clear Mike was right and had spoken the final word. We had to sell the campus and relocate, not because it was easy or financially lucrative or would solve our community conflicts, but because that was the best way to fulfill our mission for the next fifty years.

The main reason for the seminary's remarkable unity through the entire process was the communal ownership of our clearly articulated mission statement (initiated and cultivated long before the relocation was contemplated). When the sale announcement was made, both our mission statement and our code-phrase for declaring its importance were part of my speech (see Appendix 1). Here again is an excerpt from the conclusion of my land sale announcement, which illustrates how vital this shared commitment to our mission had become.

Today, you are part of one of the boldest moves by any seminary in the past century. We are selling a campus, not closing our doors. We are relocating and repositioning for future success, not abandoning our vision. We are sacrificing short-term comfort for long-term fulfillment of our mission. We are positioning ourselves strategically, geographically, and financially to impact the Western United States and the world like never before.

We will all pay a personal cost for fulfilling our mission and vision this way. It will, at times, be scary and unnerving. Nevertheless, as I have told you on countless occasions, "The mission matters most." Like perhaps no seminary in recent history, we are standing behind that declaration with our actions today.

In my heart of hearts, I believe these decisions are right. I have agonized over them, and have come to believe this is God's path for us. I am going forward, with every intention of finalizing the sale agreement and building a new kind of seminary for the twenty-first century.

I have made these decisions with many regrets but ultimately, no doubts. We are headed to the future and I hope you will join me on the journey.

The seminary community did more than "join me on the journey." They embraced the relocation as an essential strategy for fulfilling our mission and sacrificed personally and professionally to make it happen. When people genuinely believe something must change to accomplish a mission they are committed to fulfilling—when the change really is essential—they will move heaven and earth (and a seminary!) to get it done.

Urgency

The second diagnostic question—"Is there shared urgency about the change?"—strikes at what some feel is the key issue related to making major change successfully. In his best-selling book, *Leading Change,* John Kotter laid out an eight-fold model for organizational change.[8] The first step in his model is "establishing a sense of urgency." After selling thousands of books, speaking on change around the world, and continuing his research, he later revised his model. In doing so, he put even more emphasis on urgency—not only keeping it first on his list of steps to leading change effectively, but intensifying its importance and making it a prerequisite before taking any further action. He later wrote a follow up book, *A Sense of Urgency,*[9] amplifying those convictions with a much more detailed exploration of what it means to create urgency related to change. While Kotter's research and conclusions are mostly geared to a corporate context, his strategies for creating urgency can be adapted to ministry organizations.

The first strategy is to confront the facts about your current situation. Hard data points like attendance, baptism rates, quantifiable spiritual growth markers, enrollment, and giving rates are often avoided or minimized in ministry-based decision-making processes. Some perceive quantifying ministry performance (like church attendance or giving records) as sub-spiritual, but using information effectively—even in ministry settings—is a proactive means of creating urgency. When a ministry organization takes an honest, in-depth look at its past progress, current potential, and future projections, facing reality can motivate people to make better choices about their preferred future.

A second strategy also includes using data effectively, but this time focusing on information about the mission field or ministry possibilities. When real needs and potential ministry markets are seen with fresh eyes, people are more easily motivated to make the changes necessary to meet those needs or penetrate those markets.

A third strategy for creating urgency is a fresh consideration of God's mission in light of the organization's mission. This can be done through teaching and preaching on these issues, as well as using other media to inform and educate followers. Over time, *mission drift* occurs in almost every organization. Followers and leaders alike can lose focus of their ministry's true purpose and allow their efforts to become more about meeting their needs than fulfilling the organization's core mission. This is usually a subtle change, not an intentional choice. Because it happens gradually, it may be almost imperceptible and require concentrated effort to correct. Healthy organizations lift up God's mission and continually reshape or retool their mission accordingly.

Finally, a fourth strategy is using crises to produce a sense of urgency. Be careful, though, to use legitimate crises—not something manufactured that produces short-term response followed by diminished trust over time. When followers feel manipulated—like by leaders who repeatedly claim financial exigency and demand increased giving—they lose confidence in their leaders and their response rate to those kinds of appeals will lag. They may become so jaded they will not be motivated when a real crisis happens.

A better application of how crises can create urgency is using positive events, like the selection of a new leader, to reinvigorate an organization and move it into major change. When a new leader arrives, there is often openness to major change—even an assumption it is part of a new leader's mandate. Another application of this principle is using legitimate crises caused by outside forces (natural disasters, stock market plunges, political upheavals, etc.) to create urgency and produce greater openness to change. When these events happen, they motivate major change by reprioritizing organizational mission as a central feature of formulating a response.

Trust

The third diagnostic question—"Is relational trust high enough to sustain the change?"—addresses the confidence followers have in their leaders, and vice versa. Most discussions of relational trust in organizations focus on leaders gaining the trust of their followers. This is certainly a priority, but trust must flow multiple ways for major change to happen. The interrelational phrases in Rost's leadership definition—*among leader and followers* and *mutual purposes*—speak to the multilateral nature of leadership relationships. In short, the trust has to flow many directions—from leaders to followers, followers to leaders, among the leadership team, and among the followers themselves.

Leaders must earn their followers' trust before asking them to undertake major change. Followers must trust their leaders in proportion to the change being proposed before they will take the risks needed to get it done. Leaders gain trust in two primary ways: *sacrificial service* and *demonstrated competence*. Both rest on a foundation of character qualities like integrity and transparency.

Sacrificial Service

When Jesus said, "the greatest among you will be your servant" (Matt. 23:11), he revealed the secret to achieving greatness with followers: serve them. A few years ago, a younger pastor shared his dream for his church and invited my input. He rolled out a comprehensive vision involving new facilities, staff expansion, community improvement, and global impact. It was well-written, beautifully illustrated, and compellingly presented by a passionate, gifted young man. When he finished, he asked, "So, what should I do first?"

My answer was short and direct, "Go home and marry and bury some people." He looked baffled, paused thoughtfully, then said, "I don't know what you mean. What does that have to do with my vision?" I explained, "You are twenty-six years old and have been a pastor for less than a year. You are planning to ask people for millions of dollars and thousands of hours. If you want people to devote a significant portion of their productive lives to helping you fulfill this vision, they need to know you care for them and are loyal to them. Sit up with some families who have a loved one dying, intervene in some marriages that are on the verge of break-up, and celebrate some happy events like weddings and graduations. Sacrificially serve people by meeting their heartfelt needs and then ask them to sacrifice to serve your vision."

Leaders earn trust by serving people. Younger leaders have to pay their dues, making deposits in their "leadership trust fund" with every sacrificial act. Veteran leaders often have a reputation for service, earned by past acts, that project into and through their current leadership situation. Service stories spread quickly among people who have been cared for by a leader they respect. That is why older leaders can often initiate major change more quickly when given a new ministry assignment. Even veteran leaders, however, must continue to earn trust and gain influence by serving people.

Demonstrated Competence

Leaders also earn trust by demonstrating competence. When a leader does a good job leading lesser changes, followers are more likely to risk making major changes. When our pastor in Oregon first proposed building the new campus, including moving away from the previous commitment to not owning facilities, my children asked my opinion on the decision. I told them, "Our pastor has a track record of making good decisions. He has worked on this one with his leadership team and their past decisions have been good for the church. Based on their track record, I believe they have made the right decision and I'm going to support it." When a leader has a history of successfully leading one level of change, they earn the right to be trusted with more significant changes.

Veteran leaders, particularly when they enter a new leadership role, have the advantage of *presumed competence* when it comes to leading major change. Presumed competence is the confidence people have in a leader based on their past successes—not necessarily what has been done in the new setting. It is important for veteran leaders to embrace this concept, particularly when asked to take over ailing organizations that need immediate, often major, change. The trust necessary to make those changes rests on presumed competence because of past effectiveness, more than what has been demonstrated in their short time leading their new organization. When I became a seminary president, faculty members embraced my leadership because of my track record of accomplishing major change while maintaining stability in past settings—not because of my academic experience (which was minimal). When leaders demonstrate competence, they earn trust from both current and future followers. Over time, significant trust can be built up in reserve to be drawn down during times of major change.

Keep in mind, however, trust in leadership relationships must flow both ways for major change to be accomplished. Leaders must also trust their followers and build trust among them—meaning they believe their followers have the resources and abilities to make changes effectively.

This trust is built by treating followers with respect, speaking well of them, empowering them to accomplish lesser changes, and allowing them to make some ministry decisions. When a leader browbeats followers by denigrating their efforts or questioning their motives, trust is undermined. When a leader refuses to delegate tasks or allow others to make final decisions (even on mundane matters), opportunities to demonstrate and build trust are lost. Leaders build trust in and among their followers by investing them with responsibility and authority for decision-making, giving them incremental responsibility for ministry programs, and celebrating their successes. Wise leaders build trust in and among their followers over time, knowing when major change becomes necessary, followers must already be trust-infused so they can confidently take on a big challenge.

Timing

The fourth important diagnostic question—"Is the timing right for the change?"—may be the most vexing for many leaders who often see solutions a long time before others even start thinking about the problems. Visionary insight—the ability to see a preferred future—can feel like a leadership curse because of the angst and impatience it produces within leaders. Clear vision of future possibilities makes it hard to wait for the right time to initiate major change. Right timing, however, is essential in determining the receptivity among followers for making a major change, as well as the pace at which God wants everyone to move forward.

During my first on-site interview for my pastorate in Missouri, one thing became clear: the church needed to relocate. Their building was a small, dated facility on a gravel road about a mile from the intersection of two four-lane thoroughfares. It was obvious the church needed to be at that intersection, not a mile from it. At least it was obvious to me!

For about three years, we did various things to accommodate growth. We converted trailers into classrooms and started a second

Sunday morning worship service. When the idea for relocating was first proposed, it was rejected outright—even derided. After another year, when the idea was again proposed, there was some tepid, tentative affirmation. We set a study process in motion, God intervened (see the prelude and chapter 8), and the results validated the decision. The church has been meeting for more than twenty-five years in its new location about fifty yards from the aforementioned major intersection. In this case, while my conviction about what needed to happen was right, my timing was wrong.

Calvin Miller summarized what happens when there is incongruity between vision and timing when making a major change.

The wrong decision at the wrong time = Disaster

The wrong decision at the right time = Mistake

The right decision at the wrong time = Rejection

The right decision at the right time = Success[10]

Making the right decision at the right time is essential to implementing major change successfully. Learning to have relaxed concern about pressing problems is hard. Forcing change too quickly leads to fractured relationships and ruptured organizations. Conversely, moving too slowly can mean lost opportunities to experience God's best. Deftly adjusting the pace of change to remain in step with God's timing is a hallmark of leadership competency.

God's timing is always perfect; interfacing with his timing and timetable is our problem. The Bible describes the timing of Jesus' arrival as "when the fullness of time had come" (Gal. 4:4 ESV). The word translated *fullness* also means "ripeness," meaning Jesus came at just the right time. The word could be used to describe a pregnant woman just before giving birth. When the circumstances were just right, ripe with opportunity, Jesus was born. While he has stood crucified "from the creation of the world" (Rev. 13:8 NIV), he intersected human history at the prime time for fulfilling God's perfect plan. God's timing is always perfect.

As a Korean-Australian born and raised in Sydney, God has blessed me to live in both Australia and Korea, attend an international university in Pohang, have full-time employment in Seoul and then Melbourne, all the while experiencing cultural diversities and vibrant ethnicities.

I discovered Golden Gate/Gateway while searching for a global seminary to receive a solid evangelical, Bible-based education. God's timing is amazing. The seminary had just announced its plans to move from San Francisco to Los Angeles. What a profound opportunity it would be to serve and learn in two major cities, along with engaging with the most ethnically diverse regions in the Western world! I came to Gateway because we were moving, to be part of this great journey God has allocated to us.

For students, the move was a great opportunity, but also came with high costs. Student communities were disbanded, new student housing was in a less appealing neighborhood than at the old campus, and the identity change created confusion. We had to work through our pain, fear, and sense of abandonment—but I do not wish to dwell on these. The focus must be put on the dedicated and resilient faculty, staff, and students who accelerated the process of establishing these new opportunities.

This time of change taught me that student communities are not formed through the guidance of an administration; rather, they are organic entities transpiring from responsible members of the student body. Times of change require responsibility from all members of the organization.

God has been faithful and providential to all of us at Gateway. During a time of great change, seminary leaders taught us by example how to trust God for the arduous task of serving him in our generation.

Daniel Choi

Leaders must learn to stay in step with God's timing. For many years, relocating our seminary had been discussed and even strategized. Multiple strategic plans, dating back to the 1980s, outlined possible steps to making it happen. Every attempt prior to 2014 had been thwarted. As we look back, we now see how the timing for the relocation was optimal—based on the coalescing of both internal and external circumstances. In 2014, the seminary had a veteran president with a proven track record of trustworthy leadership, an outstanding administrative team well-suited to the unique challenges of relocation, a forward-thinking faculty committed to the school's mission, educational delivery systems (regional campus system and online program) largely impervious to negative impact from the relocation, and board members with the wisdom and expertise to keep everyone accountable to a reasonable relocation plan. Externally, real estate and investment markets were favorable, denominational support was strong, and outside distractions were minimal. While previous generations pondered the idea of relocation, it was only possible in God's timing when a myriad of circumstances largely outside our control came together at the right time.

Another timing issue related to major change is being ready to move forward—often quickly and decisively—when opportunity presents itself. A church-planting pastor led his church to the brink of purchasing their first facility. Their leadership team was unified, but at the last minute the pastor made a public about-face and backed away from the decision. His leadership team lost confidence in him for what they perceived as cowardice in a critical moment. Within a short time, the church disbanded.

In another instance, a church refused to enlarge their facilities when presented with a golden opportunity to do so. Despite their leaders' best efforts, the congregation refused to seize the day and press forward. In both of these cases, unbeknownst to the persons making the final decision, individuals were prepared to make very large gifts to sustain the changes. And, in both cases, the donors diverted those funds to other projects outside their churches. When it is time to move forward, *move forward!* Failure to do so can be catastrophic as ministries lose momentum, followers lose confidence in leaders, and resources are diverted to other projects.

Completion

The final question to answer when diagnosing the need for major change—"Am I willing to see the change to completion?"—is a gut-check for every leader. Major change takes time—often years—to plan, execute, and fully implement. The onerous part of major change is not the dreaming or launch phases; it is the completion phase.

This is a tough issue because, in most cases, leaders need to finish the major changes they initiate. There are exceptions—circumstances can change significantly while implementing a major change—but leaders must be cautious when considering leaving prior to completing a major change. They must be sure they are leaving at God's direction—not out of frustration or burnout or to enjoy greener pastures. They must be sure they can leave without jeopardizing successful completion of the change.

During the relocation of the church in Missouri, God directed me to leave and plant a church in Oregon. We had purchased the land, paid it off, and saved about 25 percent of the money for building the new campus when it became clear to me it was time to leave. The decision was a struggle, but the church's leaders released me with their blessing. This does not mean no one was disappointed or hurt in the process. In hindsight, it is clear it was the right decision, but it was still difficult for people who had invested so much time and money in the project. My leaving happened at a "pause point" in the relocation while the church focused on prolonged fundraising (since they planned to build with little or no debt). They ultimately called a new pastor, finished raising the money, and built the new campus—but not without having to deal with the disappointment and disruption inherent in any leadership change.

While leaders may not complete every major change, they must count the cost when deciding about leading a church or organization into major change. This is particularly true when borrowing large amounts of money. The religious landscape is littered with debt-shackled churches paying off empty buildings resulting from a pastor leaving for a more lucrative opportunity. Leaders must have the integrity and durability to pay off debt obligations their organizations incur under their direction.

Another aspect of completing a major change is recognizing when it is actually finished. In the case of relocating the seminary, after we moved into the new facility, many people asked me how it felt to be finished with the project. They meant well, but their question revealed their limited understanding of leading major change. When the physical relocation was over, we still had at least two more years of hard work stabilizing operations to a "new normal." We had to work the bugs out of the Ontario facility, finish construction of the Fremont campus, stabilize our finances (including managing a significantly larger endowment), settle people into new organizational procedures, revise carry-over practices that were now ineffective, establish our new brand, rebuild enrollment, and on and on and on. Leaders understand full implementation of major changes takes a lot longer than most people realize.

Leaders must allocate emotional and physical energy to cover the duration of the project. Many leaders run out of energy before a major change is fully implemented. For example, many pastors resign shortly after completion of a major building program. They allocate energy to get the job done—and then *they* are done. They forget the job was not building a new facility, it was reaching the people to fill up (and possibly pay for) the new facility. A wise leader recognizes the duration of a major project may last several years after the ribbon-cutting ceremony or celebratory banquet. Leaders count the true cost and have a reasonable plan for sustained effort over the full duration of a major change. When this is done well, major change becomes a significant milestone in your leadership legacy, not a millstone that drags it down.

From Change to Transition

These diagnostic questions provide a framework for considering when to lead a major change in a ministry organization. These are questions to ponder in prayer and dialogue with other leaders on your team. They can also guide in gathering information from employees, members, or other constituents. These questions help move the decision about leading major change from a purely subjective experience ("it just feels like something we should do") to a more objective analysis of the factors involved in the decision. Wise use of these questions—both in personal reflection and discussion with others—can provide a framework for discovering God's direction on leading your ministry through major change.

We have now considered three important foundation stones for leading major change: defining change and what it means to lead major change; the necessity of major change and spiritual insights about leading it; and diagnosing when to initiate major change. The final foundation stone is understanding how major change impacts followers and learning the skills to guide them through transition. Let's turn our attention to that final issue, and then begin erecting a model for leading major change on this four-fold foundation.

4

Leading People through Transition

"I t isn't the changes that do you in, it's the transitions."[11] This is the eye-opening first line of the bestselling book, *Managing Transitions,* by William Bridges. His book has been a "transition Bible," helping me guide people through transition in three different organizations going through major change. Change forces people into transition. Good leaders help people understand how and why this happens, as well as how to navigate transition while experiencing major change. Bridges' insights have significantly contributed to my understanding of how to do this more effectively in ministry organizations.

Change Is Different than Transition

Foundational to helping people through major change is this seminal idea: change is different than transition. Change is the new circumstances introduced into organizational life, i.e., a new staffing plan going into effect on a specific date. Transition, on the other hand, is the emotional, psychological, and spiritual adjustments people go through when change is implemented. While change happens at a fixed point in time (the week people move into a new facility), transition takes place over time (the months it takes for people to feel comfortable in their new environment). While change is definitive, transition is more fluid. Change happens the day a new pastor arrives, but transition is the up-and-down adjustment period over the following months as people work through establishing relationships with a new spiritual leader. Change is an action or event; transition is a process.

Leaders make a fundamental mistake by putting too much emphasis on change and not nearly enough emphasis on transition. The hardest part of leading major change is really leading major *transition*. Leaders with a "Well, that's that!" attitude about change lack maturity and an understanding of how people experience transition. Rather than announcing change and expecting robotic implementation with little concern for the personal needs of followers, a wise leader intentionally guides people through transition.

Christian leaders have an advantage over secular counterparts at this point. We are hard-wired to care about people and value relationships. We have spiritual motivation to manage transition well, as well as necessary interpersonal resources cultivated through training and experience. Managing transition is about walking people through the personal aspects of responding to change. It is pastoral work—shepherding people from where they are to where they need to be. It is about communicating well (and often), helping people discover higher purposes (rather than selfishly focusing on their needs), and patiently motivating them to faithful and faith-filled choices about the future. Managing transition is a disciple-making process; it is Christian leaders helping people transform from who they are to who God wants them to be and what he wants them to do. For Christian leaders, this does not involve manipulation or self-aggrandizement, but selfless service. One clear description of our role as Christian leaders can be summarized like this: helping people find and follow God. During times of profound change, our pastoral task is guiding people to follow God in new ways.

As a seminary employee, the relocation was a leadership lab for me. Dr. Iorg was honest about counting the cost of the relocation decision and what it meant for him and his family, as well as the rest of us. The executive team laid out a workable plan and then stayed with it over the two years of the move. They gave us permission to express openly the grief and sense of loss from all the changes involved in the relocation. They encouraged us to share our feelings and support one another, while also reminding us of God's miraculous work that was shaping and paving the way for our relocation.

When it came time to actually move the seminary, the president and the other executives spent six weeks packing and unpacking, pushing dollies, moving boxes, and setting up shelving—right along with the rest of us. While doing this, they also encouraged all of us and thanked us for the hard work we were doing. As a young leader, I am thankful for what I learned from this leadership experience—from the prayer times to the sweat equity. We worked together to do something that seemed impossible.

Shane Tanigawa

Leading through transition requires understanding both how change happens (see chapter 3) and how people process change (the transition process). There are three key aspects of managing transition that inform a sound plan for leading followers to embrace major change, implement it successfully, and personally manage it well.

Major Change Causes Grief

One common mistake leaders make when introducing major change is assuming everyone who initially opposes the change is rebelling against their leadership. Pharisaical followers may resist change (see chapter 2), but not all initial opposition is a rejection of the change. Some leaders feel any opposition—like asking questions about costs or timetables—is evidence of disobedience to God. It may, instead, be a natural part of processing the change.

Leaders misunderstand or overreact to initial opposition for many reasons, including these two primary ones. First, some leaders are insecure, which causes them to internalize and personalize opposition as somehow directed against them. Insecurity reveals itself most clearly during conflict with other people. The solution is learning to live out the eternal security found in Jesus Christ on a daily basis.[12]

Second, some leaders misinterpret opposition from followers because they do not understand *major change produces grief.* The symptoms of grief can be mistakenly diagnosed or ignored if they are misunderstood and labeled incorrectly.

Change Produces a Sense of Loss

When faced with major change, the most common response followers make is best described as a grieving process. Grief is the human response to loss—particularly any significant loss. Christian leaders understand this when a major life change involves illness or death, but we need to realize that loss is loss—no matter the cause. Grief is proportional to the loss, but every loss produces some level of grief.

Most leaders think of change in future terms—a positive opportunity for circumstances to get better. Followers—while they may believe a major change will ultimately be good for them—tend to focus on the negative aspect of change. They are concerned about what they are losing in the process. When any major change impacts followers, they feel a sense of loss expressing itself as grief.

What do people lose during major change? They may lose a sense of comfort, familiarity, or collective memory. When we announced the relocation at my first church, a man confronted me saying, "I can't believe you're taking my church away from me. My children were all baptized and married here. And now, you're taking my church away from me." Leaving our former worship center meant he was losing the weekly, physical reminder of happy times in his family's history. By the time he said this to me, all his children had left the church and were not publicly committed to their Christian faith. For this grieving man, leaving the old facility meant losing any semblance of shared spiritual heritage with his family.

Followers may also feel other aspects of personal loss during major change. When a pastor announced a major staff realignment, one family was frustrated because the youth pastor their children had anticipated becoming their spiritual leader the following year was reassigned. They lost confidence in their leaders and had their hopes for future spiritual growth and service dashed. Another family struggled when their pastor announced a major building program, knowing their expected financial contribution would require sacrificial giving—meaning they would miss out on vacations and delay other personal purchases. One volunteer was discouraged when her church made a major change in its preschool curriculum. She was well-trained in the former methodology and the change meant she lost her expertise and had to learn new systems. She was angry because the time and money invested in learning the previous material felt wasted. These losses, and others like them, produce the grief people feel when they go through major change in a ministry setting.

When we moved the seminary, the personal losses among employees and students were profound. School-age children lost their friends, the comfort of known systems, and access to specialized programs. Spouses of employees lost their jobs, close proximity to grandchildren, and friendship networks in their communities. Students and employees, along with their families, had to leave their churches and find new churches at their new location. A few employees lost their jobs, ending their meaningful friendships with former co-workers. Some students had to accelerate their educational timetable to graduate before the relocation, costing them time and money, while others had to switch course delivery systems, losing access to their preferred learning methodology. Everyone who moved lost their doctors, dentists, counselors, auto mechanics, gym memberships, and favorite pizza places. While some of these seem trivial, they added to the combined and compounding sense of loss that marked this major change. Followers feel loss—personally and organizationally—when faced with major change.

Loss Is Experienced as Grief

When people feel a profound loss, they go through *stages* or *phases* of grief. These have been defined and described in different ways by psychologists, ranging from five to eight different aspects of the process.[13] Most pastors learn about managing grief in the context of helping people cope with serious illnesses and death. Wise leaders learn this breakthrough insight: going through a major organizational change and accompanying sense of personal loss *produces a very similar grief process.* When people go through ministry changes, they feel a sense of loss, and express it through a grieving process similar to the death of a loved one.

While there are different ways to understand the grief process, a six-fold model is helpful for interpreting and managing grief during major organizational change. These stages or phases of grief are shock, anger, denial, bargaining, exploration, and adjustment. They are experienced more as a spectrum of experiences than "steps." People move through, into and out of, and skip around these various phases while experiencing grief. They process losses at different rates—some quickly, some slowly, some methodically, and some haphazardly. When going through organizational change, people grieve in multiple ways, with as many unique constellations of response across the grief spectrum as there are people involved. These losses may not have the same magnitude as losing someone through death, but the way people process the losses is very similar.

Another aspect of shepherding people through organizational change is recognizing followers may be managing other losses simultaneously to the losses brought on by the major change in their ministry. For example, my mother passed away a few months after we announced the seminary's property sale and pending relocation. Life keeps happening—both to leaders and followers—while major ministry change is being implemented. When major change is introduced in your organization, do not be surprised if people respond disproportionately to the loss. They may also be experiencing loss at work, in their family, or in their personal lives, and projecting their combined sense of loss into your context.

What do these phases sound like when people express grief prompted by losses in a ministry organization? Shock stammers, "I can't believe this is happening. I don't know what to say." Anger blurts out, "This is ridiculous. Our convention doesn't need a new building. It's an ego trip for the leaders." Denial comments wistfully, "Well, you have only announced a pending sale. If it falls through, we will know God wants us to stay." Bargaining proposes, "If the seminary moves, can I continue to rent my apartment from the new owner? Can I commute and teach an abbreviated schedule?" Exploration projects, "I can see some good in developing a new organizational plan. We might finally be able to get the help we need for our children's ministry." Finally, adjustment celebrates, "This is the best thing we have ever done, and of course, I was for it all along!"

Decoding comments like these—hearing the meaning behind the words—is essential for wise leaders who manage transition well. Leaders must show patience with these initial comments recognizing they are often motivated by grief—and do the pastoral work necessary to help people process their feelings as they adjust to the new normal in their ministry setting.

Managing Organizational Grief

Pastoral Care

Leading people through transition requires more than recognizing the grief process and lending a listening ear. Leaders must proactively address these issues with two primary initiatives for addressing grief. The first is providing pastoral care for people experiencing major change. Do not passively wait for them to ask for something they may not even know they need. Create opportunities for followers to express grief and work through the feelings associated with processing the change. These may be as informal as hallway conversations or as formal as discussion or support groups.

I joined the Golden Gate/Gateway team as a faculty member during the relocation. As an alumnus, I felt some sense of loss in losing the old campus, but my grief was primarily from leaving an eighteen-year pastorate and moving my family from our home and community. Our move was a positive choice for us, but some aspects of it were still hard.

One of things I most appreciated was the pastoral approach of seminary leaders, getting everyone geared up for what lay ahead while at the same time explaining and managing the grief people were experiencing. Clear communication about the mission also helped. The message "the mission matters most" was the right theme to help all of us stay focused when excitement about the move waned.

For me, the best part of the relocation experience was the actual move. We had "all hands on deck" workdays for several weeks to set up the new building. Working alongside others, hearing their personal relocation stories, and sharing hopes about the future built camaraderie and a shared passion. Even the way the work was organized actually became a means for creating excitement about who we were becoming—Gateway Seminary.

J. T. Reed

Remember the person who confronted me and said, "I can't believe you are taking my church away from me"? Rather than defending the decision with facts and criticizing him for rejecting God's plan, I replied, "You seem to really be hurting right now. Can I come by your house in a few days and talk about all this?" He agreed, and a few days later, I visited him in his home. We talked about his family, his long-time participation in our church, and his agony at losing his "church home."

He was a retired working-man not accustomed to talking about his feelings. He surprised both of us when he said, "You know pastor, when you announced the church was moving, it felt like someone died." It was my first experience connecting loss and grief with organizational change. This pastoral care incident became a spiritual marker, a learning moment shaping my understanding of leading people through transition.

Initiating pastoral care for people in transition can involve several action steps. Talking with individuals openly and patiently about their concerns is one step. Another is sharing information repeatedly, recognizing grieving people do not receive or process information clearly. A third step is creating dialogue opportunities for the community to talk among themselves openly and honestly.

At one point early in the seminary's relocation, I invited the seminary community to openly address their grief with these words:

> We have also been frank about the impact transition is having on all of us. Remember, change is the new set of circumstances, but transition is our response to them. The best model to understand that response is the "grief process" model. We have used the six-phase grief model of shock, anger, denial, bargaining, exploration, and adjustment. I have repeatedly reviewed this model with you. I have encouraged you to be honest about your feelings as you move through these phases. Talking to your fellow employees or fellow students about what you are going through is an essential part of working through the transition.
>
> Let me underscore this. Honest dialogue—including shedding tears and venting frustrations—is essential to working through grief and reaching the "adjustment" phase. When you talk about these issues, you are not being rebellious, murmuring, gossiping, undermining my leadership, or being disloyal to our mission. You are being a normal Christian grappling with what God is doing with all of us.

Sometimes, Christian leaders demonize followers who don't immediately embrace change announced to them. They are labeled "rebels" or called "divisive." We will not do that here. We recognize change is hard and transition is the process every person goes through to assimilate it. I would rather have you express your feelings and work through them than fake agreement for fear you will be shamed for showing spiritual transparency.

Earlier (in this speech), I lauded our unity over the past months. We are experiencing unity—real unity, not the fake kind. Real unity means we share a bedrock commitment to our mission. It doesn't mean everyone agrees with every decision being made, every policy being implemented, or every personnel choice. It doesn't mean we don't feel shock, anger, denial, and would like to bargain ways to make the whole situation easier. Real unity means we are more committed to our mission than our personal comfort. Real unity only comes when people have the freedom to work through a process to get there."

Several employees and students responded to this speech, seeking me out for conversations or sending emails. Their common theme: no leader in their experience had ever encouraged this much honesty. In other settings they had been cautioned about speaking their concerns—even portrayed as disloyal or sub-spiritual for admitting their struggles. Many thanked me for giving permission for grief to be shared. This proved to be a vital step in helping people draw together to complete the relocation.

It is important to be clear, however, about the process we were facilitating. Not moving was not an option. I did not say, "Talk among yourselves about whether the seminary should move." That had been decided. The change—the new set of circumstances—was non-negotiable. My encouragement was to talk through feelings, challenges, and faith-obstacles to a successful transition. Murmuring is when followers discuss ways to undermine the *change* decision. Dialogue to discover mutual strength for making a successful *transition* is different. The former is destructive; the latter is essential for healthy organizational change.

Creating Parameters

The second initiative for leading through transition is creating parameters for followers to understand and interpret the major change, particularly its impact on them personally. When a major change is announced, no leader can fully know all its implications or ramifications. Change always includes some uncertainties as an organization progresses toward a new normal. Faced with these uncertainties, leaders can vacillate between two extremes—overpromising without substantiation or ignoring concerns and communicating nothing. Since leaders cannot predict the future or control every aspect of a major change, a better approach is needed. The solution is creating parameters for future decisions related to the major change that give followers a sense of safety.

When we announced the sale of the seminary's campus, we knew it would affect employees in different ways. We anticipated employees would fall into five categories: retained and moving to Ontario; retained and moving to Fremont; resigning prior to relocation; retiring prior to relocation; and severance upon relocation. It was impossible on the day of the announcement to know which employees would fit into which category. We could only determine that by discussing each situation individually, which could not be done until after the announcement. We knew the announcement would create profound uncertainty, and while we were unable to provide answers immediately, we knew establishing defined parameters would provide a sense of security until the ultimate resolution for each person was determined.

Simultaneous to the sale announcement, we told employees in April 2014 we would meet with every person and define their future status by December 31, 2014, with final resolution and relocation happening by July 31, 2016. Employees heard, at the very beginning, the following parameters for determining their future status: a time period for negotiation, a final decision date, and a final resolution date. This time line helped everyone exhale when they heard the relocation announcement. These parameters lowered the threat-level since every employee realized we were embarking on a twenty-seven-month process (giving them plenty of time to create a manageable life plan). Two employees who had previously been through similar experiences in corporate settings expressed their appreciation for this measured approach to handling personnel decisions. In their prior experiences, one was allowed less than a week to decide about relocating and the other given two weeks before his employment was terminated.

Parameters—dates, times, procedures, and other safety-net information—help minimize anxiety during the transition. Some leaders chafe at the need for such assurances. Leaders say, "Trust me, and it will all work out." That is an arrogant wish based on a faulty assumption about the future. Followers need organizational assurance, not personal platitudes. They know some leaders die, move to better positions, forget what they said in the past, or change their minds as situations evolve. Since leaders know they do not have all the answers during a major change process, they are often reluctant to give out any information. Tension exists between leaders who would like to share information they do not yet have and followers who want conclusions that are not yet known. The solution is establishing parameters—guardrails on the major change process that give leaders time and flexibility to make good decisions—while also giving followers a sense of safety and control over their uncertain futures.

Establishing parameters to guide people through transition is a significant part of a successful change strategy. Our executive team spent hours creating short memos outlining the parameter-forming policies for both employees and students. Good statements about parameters are succinct, to-the-point documents. We crafted them carefully, knowing we had to fulfill what we promised by meeting deadlines and resolving issues in a timely fashion. Our integrity was on the line. We wanted people to trust us, not because we told them to, but because our actions were trustworthy. We started the promised one-on-one meetings with employees the day after the sale announcement. We met first with employees we needed to retain for organizational stability, employees who were near retirement, and others we perceived as most vulnerable (given what we presumed about their personal situations). By the end of 2014, we had accomplished our goal and finalized an individualized plan for every employee. Despite the uncertainties, employees felt safe within the established parameters, expressed appreciation for the way they were treated, and in turn made significant commitments to sustain the relocation effort.

One seminary landscaper sent me an email stating, "I know my job is coming to an end when the seminary moves. I will be here to the last day. I believe in our mission. Thank you for how you're keeping all of us informed and how you're treating all of us. You can count on me." He kept his word, working to the last day as a selfless example of serving our mission, at least in part because of the safety he felt from the parameters we provided.

Strategy Over Spontaneity

Many Christian leaders equate God's direction with spontaneous insight designed to give general directions, not specific instructions. While that might work when making minor organizational changes, it will not work when leading major change. Major change requires carefully formulated, clearly written, formally adopted strategic plans.

Christian leaders are not always comfortable thinking strategically or writing "business plans." Those shortcomings have to be overcome by leaders who want to lead major change in a ministry setting. Major change requires strategic thinking, strategic planning, and the creation of strategic documents to give form to the process.

Strategic Document Myths

One reason Christian leaders shy away from developing strategic documents is a wrong idea of what they are. The best strategic documents are relatively short. They are not huge notebooks with reams of detailed plans. Good strategic documents articulate an organization's mission, vision, values, goals, action items, financial summaries, and general time lines. I learned this lesson the hard way after one of my worst leadership failures.

Before trying to relocate the church in Missouri, we tried to develop a strategic plan for the future. We needed, it seemed to me, a re-formation of our church. We had broken systems and disorganized programs. We lacked long-range focus toward the future. While moving the church to a new location might come later, first we needed a dramatic change in ministry direction. We created a Long Range Planning Task Force to chart our future, and they went to work.

After many months of meetings, we produced a mega-notebook of detailed goals, action items, budget allocations, and specific time lines charting our path for the next several years. Just getting the notebook finished took a lot of arm-twisting and personal pressure. When we presented the plan to the church, to say it was not well-received is a kind understatement. It resulted in the worst church meeting so far in my ministry. Almost thirty years later, a friend who was at the meeting confirmed to me it was also his worst church meeting in sixty years of church involvement. It was really bad! People saw the plan for what it was—an overreaching attempt to force the church into a straightjacket of future commitments they could not fulfill. They rejected it outright, with well-placed frustration, anger, harsh words, and a resoundingly negative vote.

What went wrong? Besides my insecurity and immaturity driving me to micro-manage the process, the biggest problem was the report went far beyond "strategic direction" to "operational control." The level of detail was impossible to consider in a public forum. A good plan would have contained one or two pages of goals directly connected to our mission, along with an outline of a process for the details to be determined incrementally by appropriate decision makers (as needed and as progress was made). The report died a quick but bloody death. While discouraging in the moment, this plan's rejection kept the church from unduly limiting its future options. After a few months, everyone had recovered emotionally and spiritually. About two years later, using a very different approach, we successfully started the relocation project, which ultimately resulted in a new future for the church.

When we shifted the convention from a church-services to a kingdom-expansion organization, the strategic document was only one-page—even with graphics (see Appendix 2). When we started the Oregon church, the entire strategic document was again only one page (see Appendix 3). The strategic document to move the seminary was more detailed, but not the notebook you might expect. We summarized the strategy in a few pages (see Appendix 4). The potency and specificity, not the length, determines the value of strategic documents.

Writing strategic documents is challenging because it is easier to write long documents than short ones. A longer paper can go on and on, explaining every detail and delving into interesting (but not always pertinent) information. Writing a shorter, more specific document forces leaders to write what they really mean. It also forces them to think through what they really plan to do, how it can be done, when it will be done, and how decisions will be made along the way.

Some leaders mistakenly think a longer presentation always carries more weight. Not necessarily true. Abraham Lincoln's Gettysburg Address—only 272 words—is still more powerful today than thousands of longer political speeches given by lesser leaders. Shorter can be better than longer.

Some leaders are reluctant to write strategic documents for another reason: accountability. When something is written, it becomes more permanent. It can always be changed, but those changes must be made intentionally—often involving permission from others like a board or leadership team. When a plan is written and publicized, it adds gravitas to the ideas. It also intensifies responsibility as leaders hold themselves accountable and are held accountable by others.

When people are asked to support a major change, their willingness to make it happen and their capacity to navigate the transition are strengthened by a confidence-inducing plan. When followers can see the whole picture—where they are being asked to go and a reasonable plan to get there—they are more likely to embrace the change and endure the transition. Their losses become more manageable because good strategic planning crystalizes hope and projects real future possibilities. Managing transition is made easier when change is initiated with sound planning, not just with spontaneous impulses by a charismatic leader.

Reluctance Does Not Equal Opposition

Managing transition requires leaders who can discern the difference between reluctance to accept a major change, reticence to move through transition, and genuine opposition to God's will. As a younger leader, insecurity caused me to internalize and personalize opposition, usually interpreting it in black-and-white categories. People were either for me or against me. Reluctance and reticence equaled opposition—not just to my ideas but to God who had revealed his will for our ministry. Actualizing my security in Jesus Christ was fundamental in helping me overcome this misconception and develop some discernment about the reasons people were reluctant to embrace change.

Another solution for handling tepid responses (often mislabeled as opposition) is understanding the timeframe required for making, communicating, and accepting a major change. Leaders often spend months, even years, making a decision about a major change. Once the final decision has been made, leaders develop extensive communication avenues—videos, printed materials, websites, social media posts, mass email, personal conversations, and speeches—to roll out the major change. Leaders pour their heart and soul into communicating the change, only to be disappointed by the seemingly indifferent response of their followers. Followers seldom stand up and cheer when leaders roll out a new idea that disrupts their lives. They may react with stunned silence, polite applause, or cautious affirmation. When this happens, leaders may feel underwhelmed and discouraged, concluding they have, in some way, missed the mark. Resist this shortsighted conclusion.

Wise leaders remember processing a major change decision usually takes them several months. When they announce it publicly for the first time, followers are at the beginning of a similar consideration process. They need time to assimilate what they have heard, consider its implications, and check with other people (like their spouse or trusted peer) before settling on their response. If a major change is timely, reasonably presented, and essential to fulfilling the ministry's mission, it will eventually be embraced by most followers. Leaders must trust decision-making processes and allow followers time to work through the information and reach suitable conclusions. If the decision is the right one, most people will agree with the change in a relatively short period of time.

How long does it take followers to decide to support a major change decision? Time varies from a few days to a few months, depending on the scope of the change. Leaders may spend months making a decision, but followers do not usually need that much time to assimilate the information and make their decision. Followers, by nature, want to follow. They want their leaders to be successful. They have chosen their leaders because they have confidence in them. Most of the time, once followers have the right information, they will eventually agree with the conclusions their leaders have recommended. Most people, even if reluctant at first, will eventually adopt the change and process the losses involved in their transition.

What about people who will not support a major change? Some of them may become quiet non-supporters, people who go along with the change without owning it. They may eventually change their mind, but even if they do not, they are not problematic. The man who opposed the Missouri relocation, even with intensive pastoral care, never embraced the change. He and his family simply went along for the ride—not complaining, but also not contributing. When the church moved, they went with it to the new facility. They never really supported the relocation, but they also no longer opposed it.

There may, however, be some people who oppose major change despite legitimate efforts to help them embrace it. This may seem harsh, but those followers have to leave the organization. If they are employees, they have to find another place to work. If they are members, they have to find another church with a vision more suited to them. While some non-supporters can be taken along for the ride, vocal dissenters cannot be allowed to derail major change. A ministry's future health—perhaps its future existence—depends on implementing the change. Determined opposition cannot be permitted to undermine the effort. Many Christian leaders are pastors or pastors-at-heart. We want to shepherd a flock, not scatter the sheep. People are our business, and they are not expendable. Yet, for the good of the whole, there are times when a leader has to make the difficult choice of separating someone from their church or ministry when their opposition impedes the organization's mission. Courageous leaders are willing to make those tough decisions and live with the painful consequences.

Building a Model on this Foundation

The foundation for leading major change includes defining leadership and understanding what that means for leading major change; discovering the necessity of major change; discerning when to make major change; and learning how to lead people through transition. These are the cornerstones upon which a model for leading major change can be built. The next section provides a biblical framework for such a model. After that, the model is outlined with step-by-step instructions for leading major change in churches and ministry organizations.

Leaders realize the stakes are high and the challenge is significant—but so are the potential rewards for creating high-performance churches and ministry organizations. Leading major change is a daunting task, but it must be done for the sake of God's mission. Lead on!

Interlude

Learning from Leading Major Change

Writing about leadership experiences is risky. One common mistake is universalizing those experiences and making them applicable in every situation. Another mistake is failing to evaluate them in light of other perspectives—including both the Bible and the viewpoint others may have on those same experiences. But while there are risks involved, there is also benefit in learning from leadership experiences—both successes and failures. Unless these insights are discerned, God's activity in contemporary ministry settings will never be discovered.

Recognizing patterns and learning from leadership experiences is a legitimate way to improve knowledge in any field. When it comes to leading major change, comparing and contrasting change situations reveals timeless principles instructive for leaders going through similar experiences. Analyzing these patterns reveals "best practices"—general truisms improving effectiveness, not ironclad rules for success. Though not a panacea for every problem, best practices are useful guides to eliminating mistakes, reducing inefficiencies, and avoiding minefields.

Theological Reflection

Discovering best practices in ministry organizations requires theological reflection—the ability to interpret leadership experiences in light of biblical truth and community input. Since the Bible is always the ultimate authority, learning to interpret experiences in the context of God's Word is essential. One way to do this is comparing our experiences with stories in the Bible and learning from them. This is helpful in several ways. First, we discover patterns in the Bible that shape our choices. Second, we allow biblical examples to correct us and keep us from trusting too much in our experiences. Finally, biblical precedent confirms our experiences and lets us know we are on the right track.

Discerning God's activity by evaluating experiences by his Word can be tricky. Sin-saturated thinking clouds judgment. Flawed reasoning makes it impossible to always believe and do the right thing. Yet, in spite of these limitations, spiritual dullness does not incapacitate the ability to discern Truth and apply it to life situations. Leaders can understand God's Word and discern how to do his work by applying its insights to contemporary leadership challenges.

Another important aspect of theological reflection is interpreting personal experiences in a community context. There are two aspects to this for Christian leaders: the accumulated wisdom of the global Christian community and the immediate insight of a local community. The larger community is usually accessed through media—books, articles, blogs, podcasts, etc. Every leader should be a lifelong learner, continually gathering input from more experienced leaders (both contemporary and historic). Local community is more readily accessible and just as important. It may include church members, leadership team colleagues, or a governing board. Using local community members to discern leadership principles involves processing experiences with other leaders, followers, ministry partners, and mentors. Collective wisdom about God's activity is always more trustworthy than cult-like autocracy by someone who claims ultimate interpretive insight.

Part of discerning God's direction in community has included having people who lived through each of the major change stories recounted in this book read the manuscript, comment honestly about its contents, and suggest needed revisions. Their input has produced a more balanced perspective and more confident conclusions about how God was at work in these stories. God's activity is discerned more accurately by doing so with other people who lived through the experiences.

Discerning Leadership Axioms

Reflecting on my leadership experiences, interfacing them with similar situations, considering the insights of other leaders, submitting them to community evaluation, and analyzing them in light of biblical Truth has produced a model for leading major change. The model rests on six best practices expressed as leadership axioms. Each will be explained in more detail in the following chapters. The six axioms for leading major change are:

Major change begins with direction from God.

Major change requires initiative from a leader.

Major change is accomplished by followers.

Major change depends on God's intervention.

Major change is messy and difficult.

Major change brings glory to God.

A Biblical Framework

There are many Bible stories involving major change. Some of them describe things that happened for the first time or for the first time in a long time. They illustrate how God directs leaders to initiate major change and how his people carried out his plans. They are warts-and-all stories, full of mistakes, failures, and shortcomings, as well as successes. Most of these stories illustrate one or more of the axioms in this model.

One such story—the conquest of Jericho—is a stirring narrative interweaving all six axioms.

Joshua, a warrior-leader, was charged with leading the Israelites to invade and settle their new homeland (Josh. 6–7). One entrenched obstacle to fulfilling God's plan was the city of Jericho. God assigned Joshua a major change project, conquering a city as part of establishing residency for his people. Joshua's leadership provides a framework for exploring the six axioms in the model for leading major change.

One important disclaimer about using this story in this way: do not over-spiritualize Bible stories or create inappropriate analogies with contemporary ministry problems. For example, God did not part the Red Sea as a parable for our seminary escaping legal bondage. He did not send Nehemiah to rebuild the wall of Jerusalem to model building a new church facility. Moses was not told how to organize a nation as a model for developing a new ministry organizational chart. Inappropriate applications of stories like these violate the integrity of the Bible and proof-texts in a detrimental way. The Jericho narrative establishes a framework only. I am not implying in the least it was somehow analogous to the seminary's experience. Biblical stories like this illustrate God's activity. Using this story in this way is in line with Paul's directive that Old Testament events "took place as examples for us" (1 Cor. 10:6) and "happened to them as examples, and they were written for our instruction" (1 Cor. 10:11).

The Jericho narrative is a remarkable story of leading major change and accomplishing an enormous God-directed initiative. The story provides a framework for understanding the six axioms of leading major change. Within this example of biblical leadership, different aspects for leading major change are modeled and best practices are illustrated. While various aspects of leading change are part of the story, it begins where all major change must begin—with God's direction. We start with that seminal axiom.

PART TWO

A Model for Leading Major Change

5

Major Change Begins with Direction from God

Major change begins with direction from God. While that seems obvious, leaders are often tempted to initiate major change for other reasons. They may allow personal agendas, needs of followers, demands of critics, or some other dubious source to motivate making major change. Even when leaders propose the right changes for the right reason, they sometimes rush ahead of God's timing and endure the painful consequences. Since any major change has long-standing implications for a church or ministry organization, it is imperative God be the instigator—at his pace, in his time.

Christians often speak of "finding God's will" or "getting God's direction" on decisions. Often these comments relate to personal decisions, like whom to marry, what school to attend, or which job to take. Resources helping Christians with this process usually focus on individuals finding and following God's direction. But what about when the decision is not so personal? What about situations involving many people—like employees, students, or church members? How does hearing from God for a community differ from discerning his guidance individually? Who is responsible when a decision impacts an entire group of people? Perhaps most importantly, how does God communicate today in these situations? Leaders must answer these questions effectively, avoiding interjecting their personal desires into the equation and finding God's direction for their organization.

God Speaks

The story of Joshua leading the Jericho conquest begins this way:

Now Jericho was strongly fortified because of the Israelites—no one leaving or entering. The LORD said to Joshua, "Look, I have handed Jericho, its king, and its best soldiers over to you. March around the city with all the men of war, circling the city one time. Do this for six days. Have seven priests carry seven ram's-horn trumpets in front of the ark. But on the seventh day, march around the city seven times, while the priests blow the trumpets. When there is a prolonged blast of the horn and you hear its sound, have all the troops give a mighty shout. Then the city wall will collapse, and the troops will advance, each man straight ahead." (Josh. 6:1–5)

Joshua was given detailed instructions promising victory over the city, its king, and its army. He was told to organize the battle assault more like a parade, circling the city once each day for six days, then making seven laps on the seventh day. The priests were to blow their trumpets, including a prolonged special trumpet peal on the last day, and then the people would shout down the walls before marching in and taking over the city. What a battle plan!

While those details are intriguing, the most amazing part of this story is that God communicated with Joshua. The phrase, "The LORD said to Joshua," contains heart-stopping words that should give every leader pause: *"The LORD said."* God spoke to Joshua. Every leader needs similar communication before embarking on a ministry-altering trajectory of major change.

How did God speak to Joshua? The Bible does not include that detail. The result is declared—"The LORD said to Joshua"—but any description of the means is left out. In some other Old Testament stories, God spoke through a burning bush (Exod. 3), by the mouth of a donkey (Num. 22), and with handwriting on a wall (Dan. 5). God has used very interesting media to get his point across. With Joshua, however, there is no mention of the means—just that God spoke and Joshua received the message.

Making assumptions about how this happened or pressing these Old Testament examples too far can lead to the "Moses on the Mountain" method of discerning God's direction. A leader using this tactic goes away to a retreat or conference, meets with God, draws conclusions about his direction, and then announces it to his followers—case closed. While that worked for Moses, this method only works when accompanied by a burning bush! God spoke to Joshua. We know that and are inspired by it. But leaders today should look to New Testament models, rather than Old Testament stories, for instruction about receiving God's direction, particularly about major change.

New Testament Models

The first recorded church leadership decision, just prior to Pentecost, reveals how the early Christian community made a significant decision. The problem was replacing Judas (who had betrayed Jesus), rounding out the twelve-member apostolic leadership team. Part of the story reads like this:

> In those days Peter stood up among the brothers and sisters—the number of people who were together was about a hundred and twenty—and said: "Brothers and sisters, it was necessary that the Scripture be fulfilled that the Holy Spirit through the mouth of David foretold about Judas, who became a guide to those who arrested Jesus. . . . Therefore, from among the men who have accompanied us during the whole time the Lord

Jesus went in and out among us—beginning from the baptism of John until the day He was taken up from us—from among these, it is necessary that one become a witness with us of his resurrection." So they proposed two: Joseph, called Barsabbas, who was also known as Justus, and Matthias. Then they prayed, "You, Lord, know everyone's hearts; show us which of these two you have chosen to take the place in this apostolic ministry that Judas left to go where he belongs." Then they cast lots for them, and the lot fell to Matthias and he was added to the eleven apostles. (Acts 1:15–16, 21–26)

The following key elements to community decision making stand out. First, they consulted God's Word (Acts 1:16, 20). Second, they referenced the Holy Spirit's guidance (Acts 1:16)—particularly in the context of giving them the Word of God. Third, they established reasonable criteria for the replacement apostle (Acts 1:21–22). Fourth, they proposed options—two men who met the standards for selection (Acts 1:23). Fifth, they prayed (Acts 1:24–25). Finally, they made a community-based decision by casting lots—using an Old Testament method in the final days before the Spirit-era dawned at Pentecost (Acts 1:26).

Another significant instance of a community discerning God's direction happened in Acts 15. This story took place several years after the one outlined above. By then, church leaders were learning more fully how to make decisions in a Spirit-led community context. The story in Acts 15:1–35 involves delegations from two churches (Jerusalem and Antioch) meeting to decide an important doctrinal issue. The question was the role of circumcision in salvation: was it required prior to conversion or was salvation by grace through faith (apart from any external work)? Here are some excerpts from the story that focus on the decision-making process used by the community. Note the parallels in this story with the key components identified in the previous example.

First, after hearing reports from various parties involved in the dispute, James (a pastoral leader in Jerusalem) referenced the Word of God: "and the words of the prophets agree with this, as it is written . . ." (Acts 15:15). Second, Peter mentioned the work of the Holy Spirit as part of the process: "Brothers and sisters, you are aware that in the early days God made a choice among you, that by my mouth the Gentiles would hear the gospel message and believe. And God, who knows the heart, bore witness to them by giving the Holy Spirit, just as he also did to us" (Acts 15:7–8). When James later wrote the letter summarizing the conclave's conclusions, he attributed its origination to the Spirit: "For it was the Holy Spirit's decision—and ours—not to place further burdens on you beyond these requirements" (Acts 15:28). Third, the leaders cited reasonable evidence for their decision. Peter testified about the Gentiles, "He (God) made no distinction between us and them" (Acts 15:9) and cautioned the assembly from rejecting God's obvious work: "Now then, why are you testing God by putting a yoke on the disciples' necks that neither our ancestors nor we have been able to bear? On the contrary, we believe that we are saved through the grace of the Lord Jesus in the same way they are" (Acts 15:10–11). In addition, Paul and Barnabas described "the signs and wonders God had done through them among the Gentiles" (Acts 15:12). Fourth, James proposed a solution, that the group "write to them" (Acts 15:20) summarizing their conclusions and asking for deference in matters of fellowship between Gentile and Jewish believers. This letter was later written and sent by trusted couriers on a tour of Gentile churches (Acts 15:23ff). Fifth, while prayer was explicitly mentioned in the first story, there is no mention of it in this passage. Does that mean they did not pray? No. It only means prayer was not explicitly mentioned. Note the references to the community being involved throughout this process: "the whole assembly became silent" (Acts 15:12), "Brothers and sisters, listen to me" (Acts 15:13), "it was the Holy Spirit's decision—and ours" (Acts 15:28), and "then the apostles and the elders, with the whole church, decided to select men who were among them and to send them" (Acts 15:22).

These two stories illustrate some of the processes by which God's direction is discerned or discovered in a church or ministry. While these stories are descriptive of what happened, they are also prescriptive—but not in a formulaic way. Other decision-making stories in Acts contain some of these same elements, but emphasize different aspects depending on the situation and issue at hand. Synthesizing these stories produces the following principles—not formulas—guiding leaders to discern God's direction in community and make the major changes necessary to advance his mission.

God Speaks through His Word

The primary way God speaks to leaders is through the Bible. God uses His Word to guide leaders in corporate decision-making in two primary ways. God instructs *devotionally* to "rebuke, correct, and encourage" leaders (2 Tim. 4:2). When a group of leaders are all reading, studying, and learning from the Bible, God aligns their thinking with his goals and unifies disparate mind-sets on his purposes. All leaders must maintain consistent private devotional habits and also spend time reflecting together on what they are learning from the Word. Doing this enables them to discover a commonality of spiritual understanding and perspective—what the Bible calls the "mind of Christ" (1 Cor. 2:16).

God also guides *directionally*, meaning he uses the Bible to clarify how any potential ministry decision relates to his overall mission of creating a community for his eternal companionship (Eph. 3:8–11). As previously underscored, major changes in ministry organizations must always serve God's mission. His mission is a plumb bob, a straight line that never changes. Since a "chapter and verse" reference does not exist for many leadership decisions, alignment with God's overall mission is an essential evaluative standard. The Bible does not have a verse specifying when to reorganize staff, relocate to a new campus, or revise a small group strategy—but their appropriateness can be determined in light of God's mission.

Discerning leaders allow the Bible to help them consider specific decisions in light of their alignment with God's overarching mission. This can be a purifying process, forcing leaders to consider the underlying reasons for potential major changes and rejecting those that are self-serving or otherwise fail to pass muster when measured against God's mission. When the veneer is peeled back, if a decision reeks of individual self-interest or organizational self-preservation, it is not the right decision. Major change should only be made when it will legitimately advance God's mission.

When we were deliberating relocating the seminary, we spent significant time evaluating the decision in light of our mission (shaping leaders who expand God's kingdom around the world) and God's overarching mission (creating a community for his eternal companionship). As previously described (see chapter 3), the decision was finalized when we concluded relocation best fulfilled our mission. While preserving institutional legacy and maintaining historic property were desirable outcomes, they were not our mission. While winning a legal battle would have been satisfying and reforming land use policies might have been helpful to other property owners, neither was our mission. There was no Bible verse that said, "Move the seminary," but there was ample biblical guidance for the decision. We eventually achieved clarity by continually focusing on God's mission and evaluating our options in light of his eternal purpose.

Reaching the relocation decision in Missouri followed a similar, albeit less formal, process (since the church was a much smaller organization). When the leaders agreed to investigate property options, their primary reason was clear. They felt it was our mission to reach more people, and those people needed a place to sit down for worship. Even with multiple services, there was no room to expand. Commitment to reaching more people ultimately produced the decision to investigate property options. A long-time member said, "I guess all we are really trying to do is give a new family the same privilege we have—a place to sit in church." It really boiled down to that simple statement. The mission mandated more space and the space needed to be built as wisely as possible for long-term impact. Hence, relocation was the best option. God confirmed the decision when the church took the first steps in that direction (stay tuned for the conclusion of this story later in this chapter).

God Guides through Prayer

Most teachings about discerning God's leadership through prayer, just like when using the Bible, focus on private or individual decisions. That's helpful, as far as it goes. But how does God work through prayer to guide decisions in an organizational context? How does God work through prayer in community?

Prayer must be part of communal decision-making in at least two ways. First, leaders must make the decision-making dilemma known—as much as confidentiality will allow—and ask their followers to pray about the decision. At the seminary, we repeatedly informed our employees, students, graduates, and donors of the challenges we were encountering in the development process and asked them to pray. In private settings, where information could be shared more freely, we informed our Board of Trustees of the whole spectrum of problems and possibilities, and then organized prayer meetings with them. In one particular meeting, we set aside most of an afternoon for an extended prayer time. The chairman was particularly burdened about the board praying about the relocation decision. He organized the board into "prayer partners" and encouraged them to pray with and for one another, as well as for the seminary, between formal meetings.

When we were working through the convention's revisioning, we hosted a series of listening sessions across our three-state region. As part of these meetings, we set aside time and prayed for the work we were doing together. We also had special prayer meetings with our board related to the decisions about our future. Calling constituents—members, employees, students, pastors, and board members—to pray about a major change is an essential part of finding God's direction and experiencing unity through the process.

A second way prayer aids in finding God's direction is when the key decision-makers pray together. When we were considering relocating the Missouri church, our deacons spent a lot of time on their knees (literally, those good men prayed on their knees in almost every meeting) asking for God's direction. At the seminary, the core decision makers were our executive leadership team. We prayed as a part of almost every leadership meeting over the years we were working on the development/relocation problem. We also had an annual retreat where we devoted important time to praying together—for each other and for wisdom about the decision we were making.

Leaders are typically strong-willed people. That is a good thing, by the way. They need inner confidence to bear up to the challenges they face. They are also often opinionated, more than willing to develop and defend their ideas. Leaders need a concrete way to humble themselves, demonstrate mutual dependence on God, and express solidarity with fellow decision-makers. Prayer is the means to accomplishing these goals. Prayer is more than an occasion to speak words to God. It is also how God shapes shared thoughts and brings unity to leaders who humble themselves by praying in each other's presence.

God Directs by the Holy Spirit

The most mysterious way God guides leaders is by the Holy Spirit. In the stories previously considered from Acts 1 and 15, the Spirit is prominently mentioned. He provided the Word (Acts 1:16), motivated decision-makers (Acts 15:8), prompted thoughts leading to a decision (Acts 15:28), and sustained implementation of those decisions (Acts 15:28f). The Holy Spirit is mentioned many other times in Acts—so often the book is sometimes called "The Acts of the Holy Spirit." Clearly, the Spirit played a prominent role among early Christian leaders, and still does today.

Because the presence of the Holy Spirit is sometimes connected to outlandish public displays, some more conservative evangelicals prefer not to emphasize the Spirit. They are practical dualists rather than practicing Trinitarians—focusing on God the Father and God the Son. For some, the Holy Spirit is the forgotten or ignored member of the Godhead. Leaders cannot afford this omission. They need the Spirit's guidance in making decisions about major ministry changes. This direction is accessed personally through prayer and experienced corporately in a unique way (*a signal event*, see below) related to leading major change.

All believers are indwelled by the Holy Spirit (1 Cor. 3:16) with the potential for being filled with the Spirit (Eph. 5:18).[14] Being "filled" means being influenced or controlled—hence the biblical comparison "don't get drunk with wine, . . . but be filled with the Spirit." Believers must be under the influence of the Holy Spirit, not any intoxicants or other forces. If rank-and-file Christians are supposed to be Spirit-filled, leaders need the experience even more.

Asking for the filling, controlling, and guiding of the Spirit is simple. Just do it. Make words like these part of regular devotional praying: "Lord, fill me today with your Holy Spirit. I confess my inadequacy and weakness. I need your sustaining power. Guide me today. Make me sensitive to your promptings and pliable to your leadings." When you pray this way, you are praying according to God's will, and he promises to answer—"If we ask anything according to his will, he hears us. And if we know that he hears whatever we ask, we know that we have what we have asked of him" (1 John 5:14–15). While explaining how this process works may be difficult, experiencing it is not so hard. Pray and watch God answer your prayers.

Signal Events

When the Spirit directs leaders in decisions about major ministry change, the effect may be seen in a myriad of ways. There is one unique aspect of the Spirit's leading, however, that is often evident in relation to major change. God often causes a *signal event* to motivate major change, confirm his direction about major change, or control the timing for major change. A signal event *is a supernatural orchestration of circumstances revealing God's intentions.* These events are like flashing lights announcing, "TIME TO CHANGE." Signal events have several distinguishing characteristics to help people recognize them when they happen.

First, signal events happen unexpectedly. They seemingly come "out of the blue." Second, these events are beyond what can be controlled or caused by any person or group. Third, they motivate and unify people who are awed by what has happened. Fourth, signal events are like dropping the green flag at a NASCAR race—they indicate it is time to accelerate the pace. Finally, these events become part of the narrative— a part of the bedrock when difficulty comes—strengthening faith by reminding everyone how God acted to launch the major change.

One of the most helpful aspects of signal events is how they relate to the timing of major change. Leaders often see the need for major change long before their followers. They can become frustrated with the pace of change, wondering why their followers cannot see the same needs, and sense the same urgency about moving forward. Leaders sometimes try to force the issue, getting people to attempt a major change before the timing is right. Maturing leaders learn to wait for the right time to lead major change. The best indicator about God's timing for major change is a signal event.

A Signal to Move

My first inclination the Missouri church needed to relocate was during my first on-site interview. It was clear the church needed to move—but even as a novice, I knew it would be some time before that idea could be seriously considered. For the first few years, we created workaround space alternatives as the church grew. Those sufficed for a while, but there was an underlying sense those solutions were temporary. When relocation was first proposed, church leaders rejected it out of hand. We then doubled-down on efforts to solve our facility problems in other ways. After another year, when relocation was again mentioned, the idea was more well-received.

After a few meetings, the deacons (the leadership group in that church) agreed to ask the church to elect a committee to investigate the options. The church was told about this and the vote to establish the committee was set for a future Wednesday night. Since this was a "search and study" committee only, the response from most people was positive. Those who wanted to relocate saw it as a step forward. Those who opposed any move considered it a good step toward ending the discussion. They believed once the facts were discovered, the idea would die a natural death.

On the Saturday morning prior to the Wednesday vote to select the committee, one of the men (Keith) nominated to serve on the committee dropped in on a local real estate developer to discuss any property options he might have for our church. At first, the developer said he had nothing to offer—since none of his current properties were zoned for business use (which he assumed was the reason for the inquiry). When he learned the request was for a church, he changed his tune.

The developer pulled out a drawing for a proposed subdivision, on ten acres of property, about fifty yards from the intersection of two four-lane arterials, one mile from our church's current location. He indicated he had not started the project, was dubious about its viability in the market at that time, and would sell the site to us for "what he had in it" since it was "for a church." He offered us the property for $84,000 (we already had half that amount saved for future needs).

Keith brought the drawing to my house that Saturday afternoon, told me about his conversation and the offer. We sat at my dining room table and looked at each other slack-jawed. As a young pastor trying to lead my first major change, I did not know about signal events. We knew, however, something supernatural was happening. We knew God was moving and we had to get in step with him.

The following Wednesday, after the committee was elected, we met to tell them about the offer. Keith told the story of what happened the previous Saturday. When he finished, the other men sat silently for a while. One of them finally said, "Well, it's obvious God has done this. I think our work is done. God wants to move our church." We spent the next few weeks in due diligence about the property, but soon made a recommendation to buy it. When the church heard the backstory, there was a groundswell of unity and excitement to relocate. We bought the property and raised the balance to pay it off in less than a year.

While many had thought about relocating the church for years, the timing had never been right. The church's leaders had never been unified because no one could imagine how we could afford to move. The assumptions about land costs, building costs, and our limited financial base had kept them from seriously considering the possibility. Part of the delay was God allowing me to earn some leadership credibility. At just the right time, in an unmistakable demonstration of his power to coordinate circumstances and create opportunity, God signaled it was time for the church to move.

A Signal to Sell

For more than three decades, seminary leaders had discussed selling the property in Marin County and moving to another location. Various attempts had been made by many well-meaning people to do this, all to no avail. It was simply too complicated. The various components—a buyer for the property, suitable terms for the sale, a timetable accommodating an ongoing academic program, availability of a new campus location, a leadership team with the needed skills and background, flexible academic programs to handle the transition, and multiple other factors—had never come together.

In March 2013, the signal event happened. A potential buyer approached us about purchasing the property. For the first time, we had a person with the means and expertise who was willing to assume all future development risk. For the first time, we were approached by a person with altruistic motives rather the need to make a quick profit. For the first time, we had a potential buyer who understood the importance of maintaining our academic programs through the transition and would accommodate us. Within a short time after meeting our buyer, we knew something different was happening. Our leaders sensed God was waving the green flag. It was time to get moving—and that is what we did.

A Signal to Change Directions

When our church in Oregon decided to build a campus, it was another kind of signal event that motivated the decision. This event did not confirm a desired direction, but instead demanded we go a new direction. Our church had been portable for ten years—with a stated and well-publicized strategy of permanent portability. One day our pastor heard a proposal from another pastor in our area. His idea was simple. Their church had land and buildings, but was struggling to survive. Our church had strong leadership and a healthy ministry, but lacked facilities. He proposed they give our church their facilities and we accept their members into our church.

Our leaders spent months contemplating this proposal. One problem emerged. While the struggling church had some land and buildings, their site was relatively small. We were concerned that accepting this gift would ultimately restrict our growth. As news spread about the merger possibility and the site-size dilemma, a member of our church came forward with an interesting proposal. He agreed the site being offered was too small to accommodate our future growth. Then he revealed he owned the adjoining land. He had never developed the property, in hopes the smaller church would grow and need it someday. He bought it as a "spiritual investment" and land-banked it just in case it was needed for future ministry. He offered to give our church the property if the merger was approved.

When the pastor shared all this with our church, he concluded by saying, despite our past strategic commitment to portability, "It's time to build." The church wholeheartedly changed its direction, almost overnight. Those simple words, "It's time to build," became our rallying cry. Within a year, a church with about 250 attenders committed $2 million to remodel the existing buildings, erect two new buildings, and add parking and landscaping to create a campus.

God signaled it was time to build by giving the church amazing resources. No one imagined anything like this would ever happen. When God was ready for a portable church to have a building—even though they did not want one—he orchestrated supernatural circumstances to make it happen. Signal events pave the way for major change, confirm the timing of major change, and unify people around making major change. When God is ready for a major change to happen, he signals his will in unmistakable ways.

When discerning whether to initiate a major change, look for a signal event. While they are not required and do not always happen as dramatically as in these stories, they can be helpful in discovering God's direction and timing. Signal events are helpful ways God green-lights major change.

God Communicates through People

Organizational decision-making involves making choices that impact entire communities. Since implementing major change requires involving many people (see chapter 7), decisions to launch major change are best made by those who will be involved in the implementation.

There are two primary groups to involve in making a decision to lead major change.

Colleagues

The first group for leaders to consult are colleagues—fellow leaders who bear responsibility for implementing the major change. They are the people—in whatever office or title—charged with the leadership of a church or organization. In the Missouri church, they were a small paid staff and some key volunteers. In the convention, they were the director-level employees. When we started the new church, it was me and another pastor—along with an elder-like leadership group that formed in the first year. At the seminary, my leadership colleagues include the vice presidents, who comprise an executive leadership team. In every healthy ministry context, there is a clearly defined leadership group who has administrative oversight. Good decisions about major change, along with its implementation, depend on groups like these functioning effectively.

Collegial decision-making contributes to good decisions about major change in several ways. First, a leadership group creates more ideas and options about a major change than any one person can produce. Second, a group can also edit out bad ideas, eliminating them before they do any damage by public disclosure. Third, good ideas can be turned into great ideas as the leadership group sharpens them. Fourth, objections from group members to a major change are usually the same as will be faced when the issue becomes public. Solving these problems in private may eliminate the issue as a concern, give leaders time to think through appropriate responses prior to going public, and allow leaders to practice dialoging about troublesome issues. Finally, a group decision—particularly when one or more people are reluctant to go forward—can be the means God uses to keep a major change on his timetable.

While leaders may be frustrated when ideas are not immediately embraced or hit various roadblocks, the best decisions—in quality and

timing)—almost always coincide with a leadership team becoming unified. When this happens at the seminary, we propose better options, we
have fewer questions from our board, and we have less opposition from
our constituents. When we communicate unified decisions, it increases
our confidence (which becomes contagious) and diminishes anxiety
about publicizing the decision (since there are far fewer unanticipated
questions when this healthy process has been followed).

Group decisions promote wisdom. "Listen to advice and accept
instruction, that you may gain wisdom in the future" (Prov. 19:20 ESV).
They also lead to success. "Plans fail when there is no counsel, but with
many advisors they succeed" (Prov. 15:22). Paul usually traveled with a
team and often wrote using the pronouns "we" or "us"—not just as a
literary device, but as a statement of collective leadership (2 Cor. 1:6–10;
1 Cor. 4:1). In most cases where elders or apostles are mentioned in the
New Testament, they are mentioned in the plural, focusing more on
their group identity than their individual office. Learning to lead with
colleagues accelerates leadership influence, improves decision-making,
and makes it possible to lead major change more effectively. At the
seminary, the men listed on the dedication page put their families,
reputations, and careers on the line when they stood together to create
Gateway Seminary. We did together what no one could have done alone.

Authorities

The other group to consult when deciding about leading major
change is authorities. There are many different models of authority structures in churches and ministry organizations. Every leader is
accountable to a church, a group of elders, a bishop, a board, or some
other authority. When leading major change, because of the scope and
impact of the change, those with ultimate authority must make the
final decision. In my congregationally governed church experiences,
the Missouri church voted to relocate (recommended by the deacons)
and the Oregon church voted to build a campus (recommended by the

leadership team). In both the convention and the seminary, the respective boards made the final decisions about revisioning and relocating, about reorganizing and renaming. Wise leaders know to whom they are accountable and who has ultimate authority in their church or ministry organization. Rather than circumvent authority structures, wise leaders engage them and use them appropriately to make better decisions.

Much of the previous counsel related to colleagues also applies to authorities. Depending on the authority structure and how decisions are made, however, authorities will likely be less involved in the recommendation process than colleagues. They can still be vital sources of information and counsel during the deliberative period leading to a decision. Whether they are engaged through surveys (like the membership of a church) or discussion groups (like a monthly elders meeting), their input can shape the content, direction, and timing of a major change. Ultimately, their chief role is making the final decision by determining and interpreting God's direction regarding major change. When they do this well, there is no equivocation in their decision, and it becomes another plank in the platform supporting the change—especially when implementation inevitably becomes messy and difficult (see chapter 9).

When our board decided to move the seminary, they made the final decision in executive session (a private meeting with no staff present). They later called me back into the room and the chairman (in front of the entire board) said something like this: "Dr. Iorg, we have voted unanimously to sell the Marin County property. We also want you to know we have made this decision and it is our decision. No matter what happens in the next few months, we will stand with you and own this decision. We will not waver. You can count on us." In the months following, they did exactly what they promised. Their decision and their resolve steeled me during trying times.

God has created authority structures for our good. They bring a needed check-and-balance to organizational decision-making. They also bring steely-eyed determination for difficult or controversial decisions.

Leaders who learn to work well under authority find comfort and strength in group decisions affirming God's direction—particularly when leading major change.

When I became a trustee at Golden Gate/Gateway, the morass of developing the property and dealing with the local community and government had bogged down the seminary. It took about two years for me to fully grasp the impossibility of the seminary's position. As I prayed through the issues, I asked for wisdom for the leadership team as they dealt with those very troublesome issues. During a prayer meeting at one of the board meetings in 2012, I prayed with a trustee/alumni and he prayed the Lord would lead us away from Mill Valley. His prayer helped show me the direction we needed to take.

The meeting in which we finally decided to sell the property will be etched in my mind forever. Dr. Iorg presented the issues; we asked a number of questions; we had thorough discussion; and then Dr. Iorg and the rest of the staff left the room. The board was silent for a moment. Someone led us in prayer. Then Milton Higgins (who had been a student in the first class in Mill Valley in 1959) made a motion to approve all five proposals empowering the property sale, name change, and relocation. Someone seconded it. Chairman Steve Sheldon asked if there was discussion. We were silent. No discussion. There was a sense the Lord was in this. Then someone called for a vote. We voted by secret ballot on all five motions and all were unanimous.

I have been in a lot of meetings, church and otherwise. Unanimity is rarely achieved. Some acquiesce but do so with inner reservations. None of us had reservations. After the vote, the only response any of us expressed was awe at being a part of what the Lord had done.

Keith Goeking

Get Moving

God speaks to leaders in and through authority structures. That is an amazing reality and a tremendous source of confidence for leaders contemplating major change. God wants his work done well, much more so than any earthly leader. God longs to communicate through his Word to praying leaders who submit themselves to the Spirit's guidance and draw on the wisdom of fellow leaders. Before launching any major change, make sure you have a settled conviction about God's direction. Then, once God speaks, get moving!

6

Major Change Requires Initiative from a Leader

Leading major change requires initiative from a leader who will champion the change. Someone must take responsibility to envision, strategize, implement, and complete a major change, or it will not happen. Aspects of innovation may be managed by employees or volunteers, but a dream is usually birthed in the mind of an individual who then becomes its passionate advocate. Even when an idea emerges from a group, some leader has to own it personally and commit to it fully before real progress will be made.

Strong leaders are sometimes devalued by people who equate strong-minded intentionality with boorish behavior. The former is possible without the later. Christian leaders are sometimes reluctant to exert themselves, lest they be seen as self-promoting or arrogant. They value meekness and gentleness as fruit of the Spirit, but then wonder how to reconcile those attributes with the bold confidence needed to lead major change. The tension between stepping forward and serving humbly can be paralyzing. These misunderstandings must be overcome by leaders who lead major change. Real change requires a point person who will pay the price to make it happen.

God Starts by Selecting a Leader

Throughout the Bible, when God was ready to do something new, he started by choosing a leader—Abraham inaugurated a nation; Moses led the Israelites out of slavery; Nehemiah rebuilt the wall around Jerusalem; Peter led the disciples who guided the early church; and Paul expanded the gospel among the Gentiles. God assigns leaders, then uses them to accomplish his purposes. When an organization needs major change, God usually begins the process by placing the right person at the helm. He has an uncanny way of placing leaders with the right gift mix, life background, professional experiences, and leadership training to do what needs to be done. An organization's leader has a profound impact on the kind of major changes it makes, the pace of those changes, and the way the changes will be done. For all these reasons, leadership selection is a vital precursor to major change.

If you are a leader, your assignment is significant. God has placed you—with your unique skill set—in a ministry that needs what you have to offer. If you are a member of an organization that needs major change, make sure you have the right leader before attempting those changes. Major change starts with having the right leader.

God installed Joshua as the leader who would conquer Jericho. "Moses my servant is dead. Now you and all the people prepare to cross over the Jordan. . . . I will be with you, just as I was with Moses" (Josh. 1:2, 5). Moses had been a deliverer; Joshua was a warrior. One skill set was needed to deliver the Hebrews from Egypt, another to lead them to conquer their new homeland. While different challenges require different kinds of leaders, this example—and countless others throughout the Bible—underscores several important principles in leadership selection. The first is this: leader before strategy.

Leader before Strategy

Some ministry organizations make the mistake of developing their strategy and then searching for the ringleader to implement it. That's a "cart-before-the-horse" mistake that ignores the biblical pattern. God's method is leader first, strategy second. Ministries must first identify the character qualities, skill sets, life and professional experiences, and training essential for a person to be successful in their context. Once God has led an organization to put the right leader is in place, he will work through them to develop a strategy for major change. The right leader must be in place before the right strategy can be developed.

Two other aspects of leadership selection processes in the Bible are encouraging—particularly in light of the inadequacies found in every leader. First, God chooses flawed people as leaders. The weaknesses (and even heinous sins) of biblical leaders are painfully evident. God chose people and used them in spite of their shortcomings. He still does this, which is good news for leaders who are honest about their inadequacies and wonder how God could use them to do anything. This is also instructive for organizations searching for leaders. There is no perfect leader, just the right leader—warts and all—for a particular time in every ministry.

Second, God patiently trains people for the leadership roles he assigns, and then uses their unique qualities (including their shortcomings) to accomplish his purposes. For example, Peter's formative experiences are chronicled in the Gospels. His mistakes are legendary—correcting Jesus (Matt. 16:22–23), denying him (Luke 22:54–62), and on and on. The results of his training are evident in his ministry throughout the first part of the book of Acts and later in his letters.[15] Similarly, Paul was sidelined for the first few years after his conversion. He went through a period of seasoning and reflection before being added to the leadership team at Antioch (Gal. 1:15–24; Acts 11:25–26). His unique background and training made him the perfect means for starting churches and writing much of the New Testament as letters to those churches or their leaders.

God chooses flawed people as leaders. He puts each of them through an individualized program to produce the person he needs for each particular leadership setting. The training he provides shapes them for future service, often in ways they never imagined and in roles they never anticipated.

Before undertaking major change, get the right leader in place. This person will not be perfect, but will have a constellation of skills, training, and experiences making them uniquely suited for the task at hand. If you are one of those God-selected leaders, have confidence in God's placement and bring all of who you are to the task at hand. You are just the person God needs to bring about the major change he desires.

Character Over Skills

Biblical stories of leadership selection also illustrate a second important principle: character over skills. When a leader is selected, the future challenges in a church or organization cannot be predicted precisely. While obvious problems may be easy to spot, others will arise that surprise both leaders and followers. For that reason, strength of character must be prioritized over skill assessment in selecting Christian leaders.

Do not misread that observation. Leadership skills are vitally important, just not as important as continuing spiritual maturity and character development. Teachability—an innate curiosity and capacity to learn new things and adapt—is more important than a fixed set of rigid, already established leadership practices. The capacity to acquire new tools is more important than bringing a prescribed tool kit to the task. Peter and Paul were lifelong learners who adjusted their convictions and skill sets as God directed them. Peter's encounter at Cornelius' house, in which he became convinced God had extended the gospel to the Gentiles, is a good example (Acts 10). As a Jewish leader, he had deeply ingrained prejudices against other people claiming a relationship with God. His vision of sheets full of animals, coupled with angelic commentary, reshaped his thinking and made him an advocate for Gentile conversion. Peter referenced this experience when he joined Paul in defending salvation by grace through faith at the Jerusalem Council (Acts 15:7).

Leading major change requires skills which can be acquired. Leaders who attempt major change need strength of character (including humility to learn necessary skills) to sustain them through the process. Good leaders learn while leading, continually discovering and sharpening the skills necessary to do the job—which leads to the next principle.

Experience Shapes Usefulness

A third key principle is evident in God's selection of leaders: experience shapes usefulness. When God chooses a leader, it is in the context of that person's past life and professional experiences. Peter had operated a large commercial fishing business with multiple boats and business partners (Luke 5:1–11). Some of those experiences were transferable to his new role as leader of the Twelve (Luke 5:10). Paul had been a religious leader, trained in the finest educational program of his era. He was well-suited for the teaching and writing ministry to which he was called.

God chooses leaders with experiences that make them useful for future service. Many leadership experiences, particularly when a wise leader discerns and learns principles and patterns from them, are transferable from one vocational field to another or from one ministry setting to another. These experiences become a resource for creating future strategies and solving complicated problems.

My experiences in moving a church, revisioning a convention and relocating its operations, and building a new church campus were important to the seminary's board when they considered me as a presidential candidate in 2004. They knew the seminary's land use issues would come to a head in 2009 when the master plan entitlements expired. No one knew what would need to be done at that time, but all knew the incoming president would have to solve the property issues. My leadership experiences included dealing with land use challenges, managing developers, and handling public and political aspects of land development processes. They also included leading Christians to embrace change and sacrifice for it to happen, as well as managing complex relocation steps, helping people move through their transition-induced grief, and coordinating ministry staff so they stayed focused on essential tasks during organizational upheaval.

God has a remarkable capacity to use leaders in their current ministry context, while simultaneously training them for future challenges only he knows are coming. Many times during the seminary's relocation, my leadership decisions were intuitive because of past experiences. Those insights—knowing what to do but not sure how I knew it—resulted from God shaping me through similar situations over the years.

When God is ready to lead a major change in a church or ministry organization, his first step is installing the right leader—a person with strong character, adequate skills, and formative experiences preparing them for the task. If you are one of those leaders, reflect on how God has shaped your character to prepare you for your current assignment. Remember, habitually learning new skills is more important than the skills you already have. Allow your experiences to shape and motivate you to do your best at the job currently assigned. God places leaders with the right constellation of qualities to lead his work appropriately. Accept that reality and move forward with confidence.

Leaders Must Lead

When it came time to conquer Jericho, Joshua received specific instructions from God (see chapter 5). He then assembled the people and said, "'Take up the ark of the covenant and have seven priests carry seven trumpets in front of the ark of the LORD.' He said to the troops, 'Move forward, march around the city, and have the armed men go ahead of the ark of the LORD'" (Josh. 6:6b–7). Joshua then laid out the rest of the plan, including the marching orders, the use of the trumpets, and the final plan for the seventh day.

Joshua personally supervised the attack. On the first day, he "got up early" (Josh. 6:12) to make sure his instructions were followed. He stayed engaged daily and prior to the final attack, "Joshua said to the troops, 'Shout! For the LORD has given you the city'" (Josh. 6:16). He then gave additional instructions about destroying the city entirely, except for sparing Rahab and her family. He warned the people of impending destruction on anyone who violated the ban and took booty for personal use (Josh. 6:17–19). The consequences of ignoring those instructions were devastating (see chapter 10).

Leaders lead. They take initiative. They stand up at the appropriate time, give definitive direction, and supervise the job to completion. In the stories previously referenced as examples of decision-making leading to major change (Acts 1 and 15), there is an easy-to-miss common phrase referring to the leader's posture. When it came time to elect a replacement apostle, Peter "stood up among the brothers and sisters" (Acts 1:15). During the debate in Jerusalem, Peter "stood up and said to them" (Act 15:7 ESV). The words *stood up* call attention to Peter taking initiative—standing up in the church and standing out as a leader.

A military officer once told me, "The first rule of command: command." When placed in charge, take charge. This does not imply heavy-handed, autocratic, or authoritarian leadership. Taking charge is more about taking responsibility than throwing your weight around. Taking charge is not about raising your voice, having your way, or getting rid of opponents. It is stepping forward to make sure difficult issues are addressed, crucial issues are decided, and action plans are implemented to accomplish your organization's mission. Leaders lead. They take initiative to get the job done. This can be hard for some Christians—particularly younger believers—who are reluctant to step forward and become leaders.

Overcoming Reluctance to Lead

Major change often looks easy from the outside. Armchair experts presumptively pronounce what needs to happen and when it needs to happen. Leaders actually responsible for making decisions about major change have a different perspective. They understand the cost of making the changes, the difficulties the choices will create, and the time it will take to get them done. Leaders can feel immobilized when facing the need for major change. At least three factors contributing to their reticence must be overcome before major changes can be made.

Fear of Failure

Leaders may be reluctant to attempt major change because they are afraid of failing. The major change stories in this book are largely success stories, but they were not perfect processes. Not all aspects of these changes worked out as well as we had hoped. In hindsight, it is easy to romanticize the results and minimize the struggles—particularly the personal angst associated with deciding about a major change.

When we were seriously considering selling the seminary, the decision caused many sleepless nights. For over a year, I woke up almost every night and thought, worried, and prayed about the decision. I fought these "what if" monsters: What if we fail? What if we destroy the seminary? What if we lose hundreds of students? What if our employees all quit or our faculty leaves or our alumni file suit? What if the buyer backs out after we announce the sale or the community finds some legal way to block the sale? These, and many more, caused lonely nights; my fear meter was red-lined!

Leading major change means facing the facts about your situation and the possibilities pregnant in the change. Facts are friends, but they may seem like frightening enemies while considering their implications. There is a fine line between counting the cost and being down for the count. Working through the ramifications of a major change like a new building, organizational restructuring, or relocation can be daunting.

Fears may beat you down as the possible negative consequences mount up in your mind.

People who lead major change admit their fears, face them, and stand strong because the mission demands it. The final two nights before the seminary's relocation was announced were particularly difficult. Fear reared its ugly head as the list of possibilities mentioned above—as well as fears about the impact of the decision on my family and health—raced through my mind. God gave me the strength to face my fears, bolstered by my overriding commitment to our mission. Through those nights, taking control of fear-inducing thoughts was the focus of my prayers based on these encouraging words: "For although we live in the flesh, we do not wage war according to the flesh, since the weapons of our warfare are not of the flesh, but are powerful through God for the demolition of strongholds. We demolish arguments and every proud thing that is raised up against the knowledge of God, and we take every thought captive to obey Christ" (2 Cor. 10:3–5).

Leaders face their fears and lead through them, not in spite of them. Leading major change means stepping forward, often while you feel afraid, and doing what God's mission requires.

Dreading Conflict

Leaders may also be reluctant to lead major change because they *dread conflict*. Church leaders are pastors and many leaders in Christian organizations have a pastoral perspective on their role—no matter their title. Pastors feed, guide, and protect their sheep. They do not want to hurt them. Since major change will be painful for some, the temptation is to avoid inviting trouble into the flock. There is a fine line between protecting people and pleasing people. Leaders protect followers by doing what is best for them, even when it is painful. When they only do what satisfies others in the moment, they become people-pleasers and forego long-term leadership integrity.

Mature leaders know they cannot lead if they cannot inflict pain (see chapter 2). No matter how hard leaders try, leading major change will create tension with and difficulties for their followers. Grief strains relationships. Some people may reject the change and leave a church or ministry. Others may reject the decision, but not leave the organization. They become non-supporters who go along for the ride but do not help row the boat. Their reticence slows the process since they drain resources—time, money, and enthusiasm—rather than contribute to successful implementation of the change. Still others may become opponents. They remain in the church or organization, but oppose (openly or passively) the change. Even followers who embrace the change—at least on the macro level—will feel the pain on the micro level as it impacts them personally. It is hard for leaders to watch their most loyal supporters go through pain resulting from their leadership decisions.

All these responses lead to conflict. They may lead to inner conflict for leaders (grappling with their consciences about the effects of their decision), conflict with opponents based on their reactions described above, conflict with supporters who resent the major change marring their relationships with friends or colleagues, or even conflict with God as resentment builds toward him for the disruptions caused by the change.

Dreading conflict can keep leaders from initiating major change. The solution to this problem is similar to overcoming fear.[16] Face these ominous negative thoughts controlling your emotions and make leadership decisions based on fulfilling your mission. Stand strong in the face of conflicts that may erupt in response to major change. Keep your mission in focus, move forward, and trust God to turn dreadful circumstances toward his purposes.

Personal Cost

Leaders may also be reluctant to lead major change because of the *personal cost*. Christian leaders are pacesetters who lead by example. They show the way, not just tell people how to get somewhere. Leading major change means asking followers to sacrifice time, energy, and money. Leaders make those choices before they ask others to imitate them—and it is costly. Some leaders count the personal cost of leading major change and decide it is not worth it. Those leaders doom their organizations to diminished effectiveness (at best) or dissolution (at worst).

Leading change takes time. We made extensive use of volunteers to build the new convention office/training center, both to reduce building costs and increase the sense of ownership of the facility by the churches. We used volunteer teams to do routine jobs, saving money to employ craftsmen for more important tasks. For example, volunteers moved countless sheets of drywall into place so the contractors could hang it more efficiently. Volunteers nailed down hundreds of plywood roof decking panels so the roofers could finish the job. When the bricklayers were on site, we provided two volunteers for every mason to move scaffolding, place bricks, and haul mortar. We organized special projects on every three-day holiday weekend—when volunteers were available—for two years. I volunteered as a laborer on all those weekends, both fulfilling the strategic plan to use volunteers and being a volunteer myself. Sometimes leading means devoting time to a project—both to get it done and to model the sacrifice of time you are asking others to make.

Leading change also drains vitality. Selling and relocating the seminary took its toll on me physically. The stress of the decision, along with enduring the public conflict, caused permanent health damage that impacts my quality of life and may shorten my life. My resolve was tested when my physician advised me to resign from the process. Leading major change drains vitality.

Leading change also has financial implications for leaders. They often ask followers to invest resources to implement a major change. They challenge people to give to a building fund, donate to starting a new church, or pay for training to do a new ministry program. When the seminary moved, spouses had to quit their jobs, couples had to sell their homes, and—despite relocation stipends—families had to absorb inevitable unexpected moving expenses. Some employees had to advance their retirement plans and others had to find new jobs. The financial toll was real and costly.

When leaders ask others to give sacrificially and share the financial burden related to a major change, they must set the pace. When we built the church campus in Oregon, our family started giving to the project long before the church established a building fund. When we relocated the church in Missouri, we gave sacrificially even though we were living on a modest salary. To demonstrate integrity and preserve credibility, leaders must set the pace in the financial aspects of any major change.

God selects and assigns leaders, and he expects them to lead—particularly in demarcation moments when organizational choices determine future effectiveness. Leaders are put in place "for such a time as this" (Esther 4:14), refusing to allow fear of failure, dread of conflict, or the personal costs involved to keep them from leading the change God directs. Leaders courageously prioritize mission over personal agendas, face their fears, and overcome them in God's power.

Leaders Must Take Risks

Leading major change involves taking risks. While the choices may be calculated and appropriate, they are still risks. Leading major change means launching on an uncertain course. The ultimate end may be in sight, but the pathway to get there will likely be dimly lit. The broad parameters of major change can be charted, but the day-to-day twists and turns cannot be predicted or avoided—no matter how thorough your planning process. Leaders are willing to take risks—and lead others to take risks—to advance God's mission. Wise leaders learn to manage and mitigate risk, not avoid it.

Planning Manages Risk

To ensure risks are considered carefully and entered into with eyes-wide-open, major change mandates a thorough planning process. Winging it, even couched in spiritual language like "we just have to trust God," is not sufficient. Yes, God must be trusted and plans should anticipate his intervention (see chapter 8). But trusting God should be part of a strategic plan—not its sum total. Hope is not a strategy.

A good planning process determines the following elements of a strategic plan: mission, vision, values, goals, action items, and resource allocation (time, people, and money). Major change is often expressed through strategic goals, set within the context of the mission and vision. When major changes are proposed, clearly within the context of a shared mission and vision, they are more likely to be embraced by followers. When strategic planning results in action items (steps to accomplish the goals) being developed and resources then allocated (time, people, and money), followers are more likely to participate in implementing the changes. They see the connection between what they are being asked to do, the organization's mission and vision, and God's overall mission.

A thorough strategic planning process about major change will also outline the risks involved. Good planning identifies and mitigates risk, rather than ignores or hides it. No amount of planning can eliminate risk. The planning process itself, however, gives followers confidence the risks described are both essential to making the proposed change and within an acceptable range of probability. Risk tolerance among followers is increased by effective planning and communicating information openly, while at the same time challenging followers that "living by faith" is a required component of Christian ministry.

Planning Increases Trust

Another aspect of risk management is earning the trust of followers through adequate planning. Other aspects of gaining trust before leading major change have already been described (see chapter 4). In addition to those, a well-managed strategic planning process, coupled with honest communication with followers, also increases trust. Some leaders mistakenly say, "Just trust me" when faced with questions about a major change. A better response is, "Here is the information we considered, the process we used, and the conclusions we reached. As you consider it, we believe we will earn your trust and you will follow God forward with us." Most people, when given the same information leaders have, will reach the same conclusions the leaders have reached.

My early attempts at leading major change involved too much preaching on what ought to happen—cajoling people rather than communicating with them. Some of the resulting resistance was due more to my insistence people "get on board" than their genuine opposition to the ideas. Christian followers want to be shepherded, not stampeded. Good leadership depends more on systematic, transparent processes and shared information than lofty oratory. Sermons and speeches matter; dialogue and data matter more.

Planning Must Include the "God Factor"

As already mentioned, good strategic planning in a church or ministry organization includes the "God factor"—acknowledging some aspects of the plan depend on God's intervention. This is so vital it stands alone as one axiom of the model for leading major change (see chapter 8). As it relates to planning, however, keep the following insight in mind.

One way to include God's activity in your plan is acknowledging the need for a signal event (see chapter 5) before a change is initiated. For example, when strategizing about moving the seminary, the need for a buyer to emerge was a part of the planning process. Because of the factors previously described, publicly advertising the possibility of a sale was not advisable. The emergence of a suitable buyer required an unusual set of circumstances beyond anyone's ability to orchestrate.

God had to prompt someone to step forward and any future sale option depended on God signaling his intent by sending the right person.

When a church or ministry organization decides to make a major change, aspects of the plan must depend on God. Plans cannot be the sum total of our intelligence offered to God for his approval and blessing; they must be bigger than we can dream up or accomplish on our own. Engaging God and experiencing his activity are essential for Christian leadership. Christian planning must have a supernatural dimension—depending on God's intervention, provision, support, and coordination for success.

Leaders Finish the Job

Getting started on a major change is often the easiest part. Excitement is high and energy abounds. Staying with a project to completion is more difficult. Many churches that have attempted major building programs know the painful reality of pastoral change soon after the grand opening. Pastors are often burned out by the construction phase and mistakenly think the job is finished when the ribbon-cutting ceremony is over. A church building is a major change—but the change is not complete until the church has assimilated into the new facility and the final payment has been made.

Part of counting the cost before launching a major change is understanding when a project is really complete. When the seminary moved into the new facility, for example, many well-meaning people asked, "How does it feel to have the relocation finished?" We answered the question kindly, but our leadership team had projected the relocation would not be finished until at least two full years after we had moved to the new campus. We knew we had systemic adjustments, organizational kinks, technology bugs, personnel adjustments, and policy rewrites that would all be needed, but only evident after we were in the new facility. Leaders count the true cost—including the full duration of time required to implement a major change—and then commit to seeing it through to the end.

Once the true time frame needed to complete a major change is determined, leaders must ration their energy to make it to the end—not just to the end as perceived by their followers or the general public. Doing this requires pacing—making sure some energy is saved for the long haul. Leaders cannot simply burn through the emotionally charged first weeks or months of a project. For example, after we moved into the new campus, our leadership team kept working for months on finalizing transition issues. We planned to take time off in the summer after we relocated, not immediately after we moved to the new building. Finishing the job requires a leader to allocate energy over the entire project time line, not the perceived time line of outside observers.

Is there ever a time when a leader can leave in the middle of a major change project? Yes, but only when leaving will not jeopardize the long-term health of the church or ministry organization. My decision to leave the Missouri church in the middle of their relocation was agonizing. In my first few years at the church, we had paid off their indebtedness from a past project and raised the money to purchase and pay off the land for the relocation. The church had then decided to raise at least half the money for building the campus before starting construction.

About a year into the money-saving phase, the opportunity to plant a church in Oregon was presented to me. My passion for church planting had been kindled and the need for churches in the Pacific Northwest had become evident during doctoral studies in missions and evangelism. We struggled with the decision, not wanting to violate leadership integrity by leaving in the middle of the relocation. Ultimately, we decided God was calling us and we told the church we were leaving. Their response was gratifying and enlightening.

Comments like these helped resolve my concerns. One member said, "You are leaving us in good shape. Don't worry. We'll finish the job." Another told me, "If you were leaving us for a bigger church and more money, that would make me mad. But leaving for missions—I can really support that." Finally, one woman told me, "Taking your wife and young family from a stable church like ours to start over with nothing, we admire you and will pray for you." Another person focused on the finances, saying, "We are in better financial shape than when you came. Thanks for not leaving us in debt."

For some projects—particularly those that happen in phases over an extended period of time—it may be impossible for the leader who started them to stay until completion. But leaders must not initiate a major change they do not intend to complete. Leaders who are genuinely called to another responsibility, when they leave, must make sure they do not leave the project in disarray, incur debt someone else will have to find a way to retire, or harm their followers in some other way. Leaders must be sure they are leaving in response to God's call, not to escape a pressure-filled change situation or find greener pastures for their leadership gifts.

Stand Up!

Leaders take the lead. They stand up for what needs to be done even when it costs them personally. When God is ready to move a church or ministry organization forward, he starts by putting a leader in place with the gifts, personality, and experience to lead the change. Leaders embrace God's call and get to work, recognizing their pivotal role in advancing God's kingdom. While progress depends on God, one of God's primary methods of accomplishing his work is by using Christian leaders. What a privilege to be counted in that number!

7

Major Change Is Accomplished by Followers

With so much emphasis on the importance of leaders initiating major change, it is easy to forget this fundamental reality: major change is accomplished by followers. Leaders depend on their followers to carry through the plans that produce change. Without their disciplined, consistent, sacrificial efforts, nothing significant can be accomplished.

In the story framing this model, God placed Joshua in command and gave him specific instructions about conquering Jericho:

> March around the city with all the men of war, circling the city one time. Do this for six days. Have seven priests carry seven ram's-horn trumpets in front of the ark. But on the seventh day, march around the city seven times, while the priests blow the trumpets. When there is a prolonged blast of the horn and you hear its sound, have all the troops give a mighty shout. Then the city wall will collapse, and the troops will advance, each man straight ahead. (Josh. 6:3–5)

The instructions involved followers parading around the city, blowing trumpets, shouting, and then invading the city. The entire plan depended on thousands of people coordinating their efforts, synchronizing their voices, and maintaining discipline in the ranks until the appropriate moment. God spoke, Joshua directed, but the people carried out the plan.

After receiving their marching orders (including the warning about protecting Rahab's family and not capturing personal plunder), the followers did their part:

> So the ark of the LORD was carried around the city, circling it once. They returned to the camp and spent the night there. Joshua got up early the next morning. The priests took the ark of the LORD, and the seven priests carrying seven trumpets marched in front of the ark of the LORD. While the trumpets were blowing, the armed men went in front of them and the rear guard went behind the ark of the LORD. On the second day they marched around the city once and returned to the camp. They did this for six days. Early on the seventh day, they started at dawn and marched around the city seven times in the same way. That was the only day they marched around the city seven times. After the seventh time, the priests blew the trumpets and Joshua said to the people, "Shout! For the LORD has given you the city." . . . So the troops shouted, and the trumpets sounded. When they heard the blast of the trumpet, the troops gave a great shout, and the wall collapsed. The troops advanced into the city, each man straight ahead, and they captured the city. They completely destroyed everything in the city with the sword. (Josh. 6:11–16, 20–21a)

Over the years, leaders have asked followers to do some unusual and challenging things like moving a seminary four hundred miles—but never anything close to this. Joshua organized an army into a parade, complete with a marching band. He ordered them to walk and shout, expecting fortified city walls to collapse in front of them. Once that happened, the people were transformed from marchers to mercenaries—yet disciplined enough to spare a particular family in the melee and avoid personal enrichment during the conquest. All in all, it was an amazing plan, made all the more astounding by how it was carried out and what it accomplished.

Leaders are vital, but followers are also essential for accomplishing major change. Good leaders galvanize their followers into a cohesive force, resource and support them for the challenges they commit to overcome, and celebrate with them when God uses them to make major change successfully. Going back to the working definition of leadership (chapter 1), note that followers share "mutual purposes" with leaders. Followers are not the means to accomplishing a leader's ends. They are not resources to be used for a leader's personal enrichment or professional success. Followers are partners who depend on leaders to chart the course, but fully engage to fulfill what they believe is God's purpose for them and their leaders. Followers in Christian ministries are not commodities to expend. They are fellow believers God has provided to work with leaders in a sacred trust to fulfill his purposes.

Leading from Your Followers' Perspective

Leaders must put themselves in their followers' shoes, seeing the situation from their point of view, as they consider a major change. A church once launched a major change—remodeling their facilities and starting new ministries in their community. When the pastor announced the plan to do this, one member later shared his first thought was, "Well, there goes our vacation money." He trusted his church's leaders and believed their proposal was essential for the long-term health of the church. He also knew participating would entail financial sacrifice, meaning something in his current financial plan would have to change.

While the leaders saw the building program as an example of missional progress, the followers experienced it as a call to missional sacrifice.

Some leaders are out of touch with how their followers experience proposed change. They are so engrossed in the leadership challenges and change possibilities they lose perspective on the impact those decisions have on others. Leaders become so excited about the positive aspects of a change, they fail to understand how it will be perceived by their followers and what it will cost them to fulfill the mandated change.

God's Spirit impressed me to encourage my wife Debbie to apply for a faculty position at Golden Gate/Gateway. When she got the job, it meant we moved from Fresno to Mill Valley and I became an unemployed pastor. Within a few months, God graciously gave me a wonderful opportunity to serve a Bay Area church. We started building a new life there.

Four years later, the seminary's relocation to Southern California was announced. Since Debbie's position was moving to Ontario, once again I became an unemployed pastor. We had to sell our home in the Bay Area and move again. It also meant trusting God for another pastoral assignment for me. While this has been a complex and memorable journey, we thank God for his continuous provision—of homes, pastorates, and the grace to move twice in five years.

Bill and Debbie Steele

Most followers' first response to a proposed change is considering how it will impact them personally, their family, or their ministry involvement. They are not sub-spiritual or less committed because they think this way. Their first thoughts are not their last thoughts or their final decisions. Once followers have an opportunity to consider their response in light of their commitments to the organization's mission and God's mission, their ultimate response usually reflects those commitments. When leaders find themselves in the role of followers, gauging their response as a follower helps them remember how their followers are impacted and respond to proposed changes. Leaders will be more empathetic with their followers and gentler in their demands when they keep their followers' perspective on change at the forefront of their thinking.

What Followers Crave during Change

Many Christians are passionate about God's mission. When led well, they are willing to change personally and go through major organizational changes to further that mission. Contrary to stereotypes, most believers are not chained to the past or unwilling to embrace the future. While it may be harder for some than others, healthy Christians want their leaders to challenge them and guide them into future experiences with God—including changing systems, organizations, locations, and facilities as needed.

When people are going through change, they crave (and that is not too strong a word) certain things from their leaders, which make the change more palatable. The more significant the change, the more intensely each of the following needs will be expressed. Followers need and want clear, consistent communication about the change, resources to help them accomplish the change, and recognition of the sacrifices they are making for the mission.

Clear, Consistent Communication

Change produces uncertainty among followers. Familiar systems, people, and facilities are disrupted or removed, producing anxiety and prompting all kinds of questions. The first way this angst can be counteracted among followers is through clear, consistent communication. Many leaders vastly underestimate the effort required to transmit accurate, timely, and helpful information to their followers about major change. Wise leaders allocate significant time and adequate resources to this important task.

Good leaders plan their communication about a proposed change as thoroughly as they have strategized the change. When we planned the announcement about moving the seminary, we spent days laying out the communication plan and weeks preparing to implement it. We created scripts with common language for all written materials, short videos to attach to emails and post on our web site, and written statements to give to employees, students, and external constituents (including the media). We launched all communication to outside constituents and public media simultaneously (during the meeting when all employees were being informed about the sale). We communicated a carefully crafted message designed to provide the same core information to everyone in the first wave of media releases. After that, we followed up with the same information packaged in different forms in various media over the few days following the initial announcement. People usually need to hear the same information multiple times before it registers with them. Leaders accept this reality (rather than complain about it) and "over-communicate" (or so it may seem to leaders) after a major change is announced.

Besides distributing information, we also arranged for discussion groups immediately after the announcement, giving people the opportunity to ask questions and handle any hot-button issues or concerns we had inadvertently neglected to address in the information we distributed. For employees, we divided them into groups with each vice president meeting with the people in their division. This enabled each employee to hear from a leader they worked with often and who knew them more personally. It also allowed for better handling of specific, job-function related questions as people with similar responsibilities had similar concerns. A few hours after the initial announcement to employees, we also held an open forum with students to answer their questions and hear their concerns.

We openly admitted when there were unresolved issues and established parameters by which those matters would be resolved. For example, when we made the announcement, we did not know which employees would be moving, retiring, or transferring to another campus. When we announced the sale in April 2014, we acknowl-edged the uncertainty this created and promised to have a plan for every employee determined by December 2014 (with implementation nineteen months later in July 2016). Creating these parameters lowered anxiety and allowed everyone to breathe easier. Knowing their jobs were secure for almost two more years and that a suitable determination of their status would be negotiated, not just mandated, gave employees a sense of relief. We started having those meetings—particularly with key employees we needed to retain—the day after the land sale announce-ment. As word circulated and those meetings began to take place, anxi-ety levels declined even more. Employees knew a plan had been crafted and was being implemented to care for them during the relocation. Our behind-the-scenes goal in leading this process was to complete it months in advance of the announced deadline, giving followers even greater confidence in the process.

In a church context focused more on members than employees, sharing information about major change may be done quite differ-ently. Keep this principle in mind, however, when deciding how much and what kind of information to share: the greater the investment you expect from followers, the more information they need about the pro-posed change. While a casual attender may only need to hear a public announcement, watch a short video on a website, or read about the change in a newsletter, others will need much more detailed informa-tion. The followers being counted on to pay for the project, staff it and make it work, or otherwise carry out the day-to-day implementation of a major change need to be fully informed about it.

Initial communication strategies are significant, but continuing communication while the major change is being fully implemented is vital. After the announcement of the seminary's land sale and relocation, we followed up with a variety of communication tools designed to keep everyone informed and engaged. For the first eighteen months after the announcement, we provided a monthly "transition update" electronic newsletter with status updates, new information, and repeated emphases of previously shared information. During the final six months prior to the relocation, we intensified the schedule and sent those updates each week.

Because the seminary operates at five campuses in four states, having employee or student meetings is challenging. During the first eighteen months after the announcement, we hosted only a few general meetings about the relocation. When we did have these, we made it possible for those who were traveling or in distant locations to participate electronically. In a similar way to the written updates, we intensified the frequency of those meetings in the six months just prior to the relocation. During that timeframe, we hosted monthly general meetings to share information and answer questions, also facilitating electronic participation for employees who could not be present.

Gateway is a seminary system with five campuses in four states. While I worked at a regional campus in Arizona, keeping up with all that was happening to our school reminded me that when one part of the body is hurting, it affects the whole.

While the main campus relocated, the expectation was business-as-usual would continue during the entire process. To do this, regional faculty and staff had to be included in all that was being done. We participated via telephone conferences in all meetings, beginning with the announcement of the property sale. While the news was mostly about what was happening at the main campus, involving regional employees brought us all together as a team.

As the time for the move came closer, I felt both the sorrow and joy my brothers and sisters were living through. When I finally saw the new campus, I felt like I had been part of seeing the dream fulfilled. Being included in the process made me feel even more valued as a member of the seminary family.

Julie Hines

Once the relocation happened, there were many aspects of setting up in the new facility that required thorough communication. In the first three months after the relocation, we continued to send out a weekly "transition update" email and also met weekly with all employees. After three months, we were able to shift most communication into regular channels, like our normal employee newsletter, staff meetings, faculty meetings, etc. As previously noted (see chapter 6), a major change takes longer to fully implement than many people realize. Leaders know, however, they must sustain an intentional communication strategy to the true end of the project—not just when the major public aspects are finished. Followers crave information and wise leaders communicate thoroughly to make sure this need is met for the duration of the major change.

Resources to Accomplish the Change

Since followers are primarily responsible for implementing major change, leaders must provide the resources necessary to get the job done. Those resources can be described in three categories: time, tracks, and tools.

Time

Leaders must set realistic time lines allowing followers appropriate time to accomplish a major change. Leaders are usually impatient people. They see the end game and want to get there as quickly as possible. When asked when they want something done, their common answer is "yesterday." Leaders must check these impulses and establish realistic timetables for accomplishing major change.

When we relocated during my first pastorate, the time to buy the land was relatively short (a few months after the decision). The timeframe for building the new campus was much longer, and seemed even longer in contrast to the short time needed to find, purchase, and pay for the land. My challenge was overcoming impatience, laying out a reasonable multiyear plan for raising the money, and communicating a sense of peace about the perceived delay to the process. The decision to avoid extensive debt by having at least half of the money in hand before starting the building phase of the project added to what already felt like a slow time line.

When we moved the seminary, we announced a twenty-eight-month timeframe for the project. We determined this time line after considering all factors—academic programs, financial resources, maintaining morale (both student and employee), pace of construction, etc. The needs of students—allowing them time to finish degrees or make appropriate plans to relocate or switch to other delivery options (online or a different campus in our system)—were paramount. The needs of employees—allowing them time to make life adjustments and prepare for the future—were also significant.

Determining an adequate time line for implementing a major change is important for several reasons. First, it relieves undue pressure followers feel to get the job done quickly. Second, it assures followers their needs are being considered as part of the implementation process. Third, it creates a sense of pace—rather than panic—about the change. Steady progress on a reasonable time line is better than frantic effort. Fourth, a good timetable recognizes the natural energy swoon associated with any major project. At the beginning of any major initiative, there is almost always a surge of excitement—but no one can sustain that pace. Good leaders anticipate this and establish a timetable based on the energy level followers can sustain over time. Finally, a good timetable recognizes "life happens" while implementing change and followers will need time to absorb these challenges while still implementing the changes being made in their church or ministry organization.

When we established the time line for the seminary's relocation, we recognized employees and students would have to manage the seminary's change while also managing their personal changes. We knew children and grandchildren would continue to be born, family members would die, major illnesses would strike, children would get sick, spouses would lose jobs, and on and on. All these things happened to our followers—and some of them to our leaders. These life events take time and money to manage. Wise ministry leaders recognize these things will happen to their followers while they are trying to help pay for a new facility, volunteer to support new ministry initiatives, learn new job responsibilities, or solve the problems of organizational realignment. Major change takes time and followers' personal challenges must be factored into the time line for implementing the major change. When a leader fails to do this, the followers will do it anyway. They cannot stop life from happening and will attend to its demands. The time line will be reset whether the leaders want it to be or not. It is better to make a realistic plan from the beginning.

Tracks

A reasonable path for successfully implementing major change is the second resource followers need from their leaders. In the 1800s, the railroad industry changed American history, uniting the nation by connecting two distant coasts, streamlining commerce, enhancing communication, and opening new opportunities for both business and leisure travel. The tycoons of the era are celebrated—men like Vanderbilt, Stanford, and Gould. But the most important people in the railroad industry may have been the track layers. A train is a massive machine with one major constraint: it can only go where a track makes progress possible. No matter how powerful the engine, unlimited the fuel source, or skilled the operators, a train can only travel on the track that has been laid.

Leaders must do more than cast vision about change or passionately advocate for it. They must lay the track their followers will use to travel to the destination. Leaders do this in several ways.

First, leaders lay out workable steps for followers to make measured progress on a major change. Second, leaders create way stations—stopping points to reevaluate, reassess, and reboot for the next phase of the journey. This is essential because major change is often accomplished in stages. Followers need these stopovers to celebrate a sense of accomplishment and catch their breath (emotionally and spiritually) before pressing on to the next phase. Third, leaders keep people "on track" by laying out good plans, thus limiting freelancing from well-meaning followers who dissipate efforts chasing fruitless alternatives. Finally, leaders supply the materials—money, outside expertise, practical tools—for followers to get the job done (see the next section).

When we relocated the Missouri church, our first stop on the journey was obtaining the land. We then laid a track to get to the next station: having at least half the money on hand to build the new campus. At that point, followers knew they would help reassess progress and lay a new track: deciding to either save additional funds or borrow money and go ahead with the project. When the church reached the halfway point, they considered their economic realities, building costs, growth potential, and national economic factors. They decided to borrow money and go ahead with the project. Their conclusion, however, is not the issue here. The key insight is this: not every track has to be finished before the journey can start. The track only has to be laid to the next way station—where everyone can rest, reassess, and chart the best course to the ultimate destination.

When we moved the seminary, we laid out a timetable with a few fixed dates, necessitated because our school/semester schedule required us to be ready to offer classes in the new locations to keep faith with students. Those fixed dates enabled us to back-date and determine the time line for many other decisions and actions. Once we communicated those dates, they became our way stations where we reevaluated our progress and made course corrections. Fulfilling incremental plans as part of the larger major change breaks the change into more manageable components and gives followers increased confidence they can ultimately complete the entire project. Small wins ultimately add up to the big win.

Tools

Providing the tools required to implement major change is the third way leaders meet the needs of their followers and enable them to do their part. The right tools make doing any job easier. I have worn glasses for about fifty years and broken more than one pair along the way. Consequently, for about forty years, I have owned a special screwdriver with a very tiny tip that fits the screws in eyeglass frames. That tool has eliminated much frustration. The right tool makes all the difference on any job—big or small.

Providing the right tools for followers takes several forms. First, it includes training them on skills needed to do something new. Major organizational changes require different jobs, different skill sets in existing jobs, and different ways to function when certain jobs are eliminated. When we revisioned the convention, we had to reorganize the staff to implement the changes. While many of the desired outcomes remained the same and many employees remained in similar roles, we moved from having "directors" to "strategists" on the staff. This reflected our commitment to a field-based strategy—which we facilitated and then catalyzed—instead of a top-down approach. The staff had to be trained to adopt this new way of relating to field personnel and pastors. Training is one way leaders give followers new tools. New information is essential to implementing major change.

This is true for both employees and volunteers. Volunteers who are expected to start new programs or staff new initiatives need training—perhaps even more narrowly focused than that given to employees. Volunteers have more limited time to devote to their task, hence their training time is also limited. For this reason, their training needs to be oriented precisely to the new responsibilities essential to implementing the major change.

A second way leaders provide tools is by connecting followers with experts—both inside and outside the organization. Some leaders mistakenly think being good at some things makes them good at everything. Wise leaders know better (their followers already know this about them, by the way). When we moved the seminary, we brought in the best outsiders we could find. They were expensive but, in proportion to the total project, a good use of resources. We employed the largest land use law firm in the United States, one of the largest construction firms in Southern California, and an architectural firm that had won a national award for designing educational facilities. As we were working on organizational changes, we brought in a human resources consultant and a compensation specialist—both familiar with the market we were entering. Our employees and students (along with our board) had greater confidence in our final decisions on all these issues because they knew we had vetted them with outside experts.

Wise leaders also use inside experts, followers who can lead their peers because of their expertise and the respect they have earned. When we built the new church campus in Oregon, a construction company owner in our membership provided valuable guidance on the project. We also had a finance specialist on our planning team, along with a person who managed dozens of buildings for a major corporation. The expertise these three church members provided not only helped us make better decisions about the project, but added gravitas to those decisions when other members heard them speak as inside experts helping guide the decision-making. Experts who share your mission and vision are a key tool at your disposal. Use those tools well to shape the contribution your followers are able to make in accomplishing major change.

A third-way leaders provide tools is by providing the people and materials needed to get the job done. Moving the seminary meant moving a lot of paper. Just the academic records for former students filled forty-two file cabinets! Digitizing a significant portion of those records was part of the relocation plan—which meant we had to buy the equipment and hire the staff to do it. Adding this much work to the current staff, while expecting them to manage their ongoing workload and prepare for their personal moves, was untenable. On this project, and a few others, the tools needed included outside help to get the job done.

Perhaps the most visible practical example of providing tools was the seminary's "packing center." About twenty months before the actual move, we encouraged employees to start sorting, discarding, and packing, particularly items that were not needed on a day-to-day basis. When we did this, we opened a packing center—equipped with boxes, tape, packing labels, recycling bins, and instructions about placing packed items in staging areas for transport to their new location. We later expanded the center as the distribution point for personal moving supplies (rather than having employees purchase them and be reimbursed). We funneled thousands of dollars of packing supplies through the packing center, providing an efficient and cost-effective way for employees to maintain a slow-and-steady packing pace, rather than trying to do it all at once in a short time closer to the actual relocation.

Since followers actually get the job done, wise leaders supply the resources necessary to accomplish major change. As a leader, make your followers more effective and maintain their morale by creating a realistic time line, laying out a reasonable plan, and supplying them with the tools needed to complete a major change.

Recognizing Sacrifices Made for the Mission

Christian leaders sometimes neglect to recognize followers for their efforts, basing their reluctance on the theological conviction we all serve God, and his recognition is all any of us need. It is not. While God's approval is our ultimate goal, good leaders know the powerful, positive results from recognizing people for their sacrifices and accomplishments. The Bible encourages us to "outdo one another in showing honor" (Rom. 12:10). When leaders do this well, surprising things happen. Here are three categories of recognition leaders can provide followers who are implementing a major change.

Verbal Praise

Leaders recognize followers by giving them verbal praise. This can take different forms. Leaders can highlight successful implementation of aspects of the major change, tell stories of individual sacrifices followers have made for the change, or share the credit with followers by identifying specific ways they have made the change possible. Wise leaders report their followers' successes in public forums, like board meetings, employee meetings, and worship services. Appropriate public praise differs from flattery (which the Bible condemns—see Prov. 29:5). Flattery focuses on personal success, often without reference to the mission or God's enabling power. Flattery actually focuses on the speaker, who compliments others to gain leverage, influence, or personal reward. Genuine praise, on the other hand, not only blesses followers, but motivates them to greater service and sacrifice.

When we built the new church facility in Oregon, one couple made a remarkable sacrifice for the building fund. Since they had been too poor to afford a honeymoon when they got married, they had been saving for one for almost twenty-five years. Every month, no matter how little the contribution, they had put something aside for a big trip on their silver anniversary. God led them to give the entire fund to the building program. After their story became known, their sacrifice ignited a wildfire of reconsideration of giving commitments to the building fund. Telling their story not only affirmed their sacrifice, but encouraged many others to give more generously, resulting in a middle-class church of about 250 people giving more than $2 million over the following three years to build the campus.

Meaningful Gifts

Leaders can also recognize followers by giving them meaningful gifts. These are not necessarily expensive gifts, but are more often items related to the major change. They remind followers of their participation in the project and give them a historic record of a spiritual milestone. At the groundbreaking for the Oregon church campus, everyone received a small bottle, filled with dirt, labeled "Time to Build." That was the project's theme, and those three words carried significant weight for all who participated. That small bottle still sits on a shelf in my office today.

When we moved the seminary, we provided some intentional mementos, but those did not prove as collectible as another "gift." To help identify which parts of the building were packed and empty, and to motivate employees to finish packing, we created a "Boom" sign to post on every area that was completely vacated. The sign was a plain white sheet of paper with "Boom! This room is finished." printed on it. After we posted a few, employees starting asking, "What else needs to be done to get my 'Boom sticker'?" They competed to get them up as fast as possible. Some of those signs became mementos people took with them on the last day.

When we moved into our new campus, we created another sign that said, "This room is 'Ready to Roll.'" As soon as an office, work area, or storage room was completely finished, we posted a "Ready to Roll" sign. Both of these signs, by the way, had to be posted by the president, adding gravity and accountability to getting one. After we completed the move-in (in only eight days, not the three weeks we had planned), one employee brought me his "Ready to Roll" sign and asked me to autograph it. He framed it and hung it in his office. He often tells guests the sign reminds him of our historic seminary relocation—and his part in making it successful.

Sharing the Credit

Finally, leaders recognize their followers' success by sharing the credit for accomplishing a major change. This applies particularly to senior leaders who often work with an executive team, church staff, or leadership group (like elders or deacons) who share the burden of implementing the change. Sharing the credit means giving verbal praise and meaningful gifts to people who carried the leadership burden for the project. When those teammates are employees, it means speaking of their contribution in public settings, expressing appreciation to them with private gestures (like a special dinner), increasing their compensation or providing bonuses, and giving them memento-type gifts designed just for them. When these teammates are volunteers, these same practices (minus the compensation aspects) can also be done. Volunteer church leaders and members often make heroic sacrifices of time away from their families, companies, and recreational pursuits to lead ministry projects. Wise pastors show appreciation and give volunteers the honor they deserve.

Pastoral Care for Everyone

A significant part of enabling followers to accomplish major change is providing the pastoral care needed as they manage their transition. Remember, change and transition are not the same thing. Change is the new set of circumstances; transition is how people respond to and work through the change. Major change forces people into and through significant transition—the spiritual, emotional, and psychological processes of adapting to it.

The key issues related to managing transition have already been covered in detail (see chapter 4). Review that chapter and add insights from this one to develop a comprehensive strategy for supporting followers as they accomplish major change. Much of what is described in this process is pastoral care—providing the spiritual support needed for major change to be a disciple-making process. Pastoral care is an essential part of strengthening followers who have devoted themselves to bringing change about successfully. Without their efforts, no matter how well-intentioned the leader, major change will not happen.

8

Major Change Depends on God's Intervention

God's work requires his intervention, lest the results be only the combined product of human effort. Churches and ministries are supposed to be dependent on God, centers of supernatural activity. For this to be true, Christian leaders must rely on God's power to accomplish his work. Anything less smacks of self-reliance and smells of self-sufficiency. Major change in a church or ministry organization means attempting something that seems impossible, something that will only happen if God acts. Any planning model that does not depend on God's intervention as an essential component secularizes the process, reveals idolatry and pride, and only produces "dead works" for which humankind is well-known (Heb. 9:14).

When Joshua arrived outside Jericho, the walls must have appeared formidable. The current archaeological remains reveal the size and extent of the walls. They still appear capable of resisting modern weaponry, even more so the projectiles available to Joshua's army. When God told Joshua to conquer the city using the parade plan, it must have seemed incredible at best, and impossible at worst. God gave Joshua his marching orders—single laps for six days and seven laps on the seventh—followed by a shout and a trumpet blast. He then promised, "the city wall will collapse, and the troops will advance, each man straight ahead" (Josh. 6:5). God did not specifically say he would tear down the wall, but the implication was clear. Walking and shouting could not and would not do the job. Only God's power would suffice.

On the seventh day, at the appropriate time, "the troops shouted, and the trumpets sounded. When they heard the blast of the trumpet, the troops gave a great shout, and the wall collapsed. The troops advanced into the city, each man straight ahead, and they captured the city. They completely destroyed everything in the city" (Josh. 6:20–21a). As we learned in the last chapter, the people did their part, swarming over the rubble and killing everyone and everything in sight. They were only able to do this, however, after God's battering-ram presence made their invasion possible. When God wants his people to accomplish something remarkable, he intervenes in powerful ways to make it happen.

Miracles Still Happen

Miracles are God's supernatural interventions in everyday life. They are observable events—tangible, but not able to be explained by human agency or intellect. Miracles do not result from superhuman effort or charismatic personalities. In other words, God does something not even the most gifted or determined human could do. When miracles happen, they produce awe and reverence, causing people to give glory to God. They direct attention to God—not leaders or followers—with everyone recognizing only God could have done what has been accomplished.

The Gateway relocation and transition was an extraordinary experience. As the executive charged with handling the legal, financial, and construction details, my daily involvement enabled a first-hand view of God's protection and provision that resulted from the intercession of many people.

For many years as a businessman, my devotions included praying for God's wisdom, direction and help for the needs of each day. There have been some special times over the years, however, when God's intervention was remarkable, being clearly observable.

For many years, speculators had approached the seminary about buying its property. Part of my job was analyzing these offers. All of them were inadequate. When God brought the person who bought the property to us, we saw his provision in clear ways. More than a general sense of God working on our behalf, this was God clearly, visibly working for us. Then, after we sold the property, we saw God actively intervene on a consistent basis over the next three years.

Seeing this happen changed me. Scripture and my experiences both affirm the truth: "Where God guides, He provides." While I have experienced glimpses of that truth in the past, I had never seen such an outpouring of God's care and protection as we experienced through the relocation. Why I was blessed to be part of these miracles I will never fully understand.

                                                                Gary Groat

Throughout the seminary's relocation, God performed miracles to facilitate the process and keep it on track. We experienced God's power at key moments in ways beyond anyone's ability to conjure or control. Like turning a cosmic kaleidoscope, God coordinated disparate, disconnected events to create a supernatural mosaic, bringing his plans into sharper focus each time he tweaked the circumstances.

God uses miracles to facilitate major change in at least two ways. First, God miraculously signals he wants something done and when he wants it done. These signal events are vital to helping leaders know it is time to get moving (see chapter 5). God allows obstacles to our plans until he is ready to advance his plans. Leaders are often frustrated by their inability to remove those obstacles. They wonder why their vision for the future is stymied. Then, God eliminates the barriers to progress, giving a clear indication of his will and bringing glory to himself in the process.

Second, God often works during major change—in just the right way and right time—to make sure his cause is advanced and people know he is making the change happen. When a ministry makes a major change, it must be done his way and at his time for the change to be successful. God sustains major change by interjecting himself at pivotal moments to keep a ministry moving in the right direction. When he was ready for the seminary to move, God worked miraculously in seven ways to launch and sustain the relocation. God's intervention was essential in overcoming the obstacles which had previously seemed insurmountable and bringing that major change to completion.

Seven Miracles

Gateway Seminary began as Golden Gate Seminary through the vision of two San Francisco Bay Area pastors in 1944. For seventy-two years, the seminary was headquartered in the Bay Area—first in Oakland, then Berkeley, and most recently, in Marin County, near Mill Valley, California.

In 1959, county leaders approved a twenty-five-year development plan for the seminary's property. It was replaced in 1984 by another twenty-five-year plan that expired in 2009. During the time spanned by the second development plan, higher education experienced a revolution, fueled by technological advances. By 2009, we knew any new plan would need to be quite different than the past plans. Not only had education changed during those years, but so had the community around the former campus. It had become one of the most politically liberal, financially affluent, and development-averse communities in the United States. As a result, from 2009 through 2013, we endured prolonged political and legal conflict, along with persistent opposition from our community to new development plans for our former campus. Despite our best efforts and much prayer, we were kept from fulfilling those plans.

The situation was bleak. We owned a deteriorating campus, in a very challenging location, with significant development restrictions, and entrenched community opposition. We were on a trajectory toward closure or worse—a perpetual struggle to preserve our property at the expense of our mission. We needed a miracle—or *miracles,* as it turned out—to propel us to a new future.

God Sent a Buyer

For many years, going back to the mid-1980s, seminary leaders had considered selling the campus and relocating, even going so far as creating detailed plans about how to do it if the opportunity presented itself. Despite those past discussions, the seminary had always been stymied by a stubborn reality: selling the property, with its inherent development restrictions and community opposition, would be very difficult. This was compounded by the seminary's reluctance to list the property for sale. Doing so would have had a devastating impact on enrollment and the capacity to attract employees, as well as inviting even greater opposition from some segments of the community. Any public attempt to sell the campus would have devolved into a multi-year conflict with uncertain results. We could not take that risk, knowing it would likely lead to the seminary's closure.

While considering the relocation option, three key sale terms had become evident. The seminary would need a cash sale (at a reasonable market price), a two-year lease back of the campus to facilitate the transition, and the buyer would have to assume all future development risks. Other than that, we were not expecting much!

Over the first ten years of my presidency, more than a dozen companies made overtures about buying the campus. Some were speculators; others more legitimate Bay Area developers. All had one thing in common—they proposed some form of partnership in which they developed the property and split future profits with the seminary. Those offers were a recipe for disaster in two ways: they mired the seminary in a multi-year community conflict while permission was obtained to develop the property and they linked us to a secular company, allowing it to determine our future. We rejected all these proposals.

In March 2013, when our development conflict was at its apex, a person with adequate resources and development expertise came to my office to discuss the possibility of purchasing our property. After exchanging pleasantries and discussing the public aspects of our land development conflicts, my guest asked if we had any interest in selling the property, and if so, what our general sale terms might be. As I mentioned in this book's prelude, my response was similar to the following:

"We have three requirements for selling the property. We want a cash sale for $100 million. We require a two-year lease back of the campus that enables us to remain fully operational for two academic years. You would assume all future develop risks—no partnership of any kind." My guest thought for a minute and replied, "Would you need the $100 million all up front or could we pay half the first year and half the second year? If so, the lease back and the assumption of future responsibility are not a problem."

In that moment, our seminary changed forever. It took about thirteen months to consummate the 106-page sale agreement (with a final sale price of $85 million), including solving dozens of legal issues about selling the property and finalizing the lease-back agreement. From the first meeting to the closing, however, there was clear and steady progress toward the sale. God provided a buyer with altruistic motives, who had a long-term vision for the property that was not driven primarily by personal or corporate gain.

God sent a buyer at his time and on terms no one dreamed possible.

God Provided a New Campus

When it became evident we would likely sell the property, we had to find a new campus. Since development and construction in California is a slow process (usually five years from initial planning to move-in-ready on any major project), we needed an existing facility that could be remodeled within our two-year time frame. We developed ten parameters (see Appendix 4) for selecting a new campus and started looking at our options near Ontario, California.

Early in the planning process, we had established a relationship with a real estate broker in Southern California. We asked him to show us any available property that even remotely matched our criteria within fifty miles of our target location. He sent me electronic proposals for more than forty locations and we later toured about twelve of them. None were suitable. We were sitting in his company's satellite office near the center of our target area after a discouraging day of touring inadequate sites when I said something like this:

"None of these properties will do. We have to find something better." Looking out the window, I continued, "I want a building like that one across the lake." He replied, "Jeff, that one's not for sale. It was a few months ago but your timing is off. It has just recently been purchased and the new owners are committed to leasing it." We talked some more about our options and then I flew back to northern California. Our broker thought about it on his drive home and called the new owners of the lakeside building. Within seventy-two hours, we were negotiating to purchase that building, which is now the seminary's Ontario campus.

The building had been constructed in 2009, but never finished on the inside (what builders call a "warm shell"). The company that built it went out of business during the 2008–2009 economic downturn. The building had languished in foreclosure and bankruptcy, only recently being purchased by a real estate investment group. We bought

the building (with surrounding land, parking, and additional development lot) for $26 million and spent another $17 million on finishing
and furnishing the interiors. The total cost—just for the building, not
including the development lot—was about 15% under the market value
of constructing a similar building in 2016. We closed the purchase just
a few days after the sale of the Marin County property, meaning we had
almost two full years to complete our tenant improvements and prepare
for relocation. We met that timetable and moved seamlessly, closing in
Mill Valley on June 3, 2016 and opening in Ontario on July 5, 2016.

One of the other pressing issues was housing for students, particularly international students who depend on the seminary for housing. As
soon as we closed the purchase of the Ontario campus, the same broker
started looking for reasonably priced apartment complexes near our
new building. None were for sale. Within a few months, however, two
adjoining complexes three miles from our campus came on the market
simultaneously. We purchased both of them for about $8 million. After
extensive remodeling, we opened them to students on July 1, 2016—a
few days before we opened the Ontario campus.

And one more thing: the Ontario campus purchase included the
aforementioned development lot next door to the primary building. Its
estimated value at the time the seminary obtained it without adding any
cost to the purchase—$4 million.

God provided a new campus. He had it sitting vacant and waiting
for us the whole time.

God Assembled Our Leadership Team

God provided the right team to lead the relocation. He brought
together a group of executive leaders uniquely suited to moving a seminary—Gary Groat, Michael Martin, Adam Groza, Ben Skaug, Tom
Hixson, and Jeff Jones. Our team had the right skill set, temperament,
and attitude to lead the relocation. We were a healthy mix of veteran
and younger leaders. We had varying points of view, a wide range of

leadership experiences, and different backgrounds, along with a deeply shared commitment to our mission and to each other as Christian brothers. Our team also had tenure—we had worked with each other long enough to trust each other and served our followers and board long enough to have gained their confidence.

My leadership experience included relocating a church, building a new church campus, and relocating a state convention office and training center. Besides these facility-related projects, my background also included creating new organizations in both a new church plant and a matured denominational bureaucracy. God had prepared me to lead our relocation and create a new seminary organizational plan.

Gary Groat, vice president of Business Services, was the key person in negotiating the property sale, managing the financial issues, designing the new campuses, and supervising construction (at both the Ontario and Fremont locations). Gary had extensive business experience before coming to work in education, which provided expertise not often found on academic leadership teams. Gary's mission-passion was demonstrated through tenacious negotiations, countless legal showdowns, and multiple hard-nosed decisions he made on our behalf. He attended every meeting, sat in on every phone conference, read every letter and contract and legal document, interfaced with multiple attorneys, met with architects and contractors, and made sure every dollar was accounted for throughout the project. During the final three months, when we were pushing to complete the Ontario campus on time, Gary and his wife temporarily moved to Ontario so he could be on site every day making immediate decisions to facilitate a timely completion. Gary's selflessness was demonstrated by this important fact: he served knowing he would never fully experience the fruit of his labor. His retirement coincided with the seminary's relocation, after which he remained in the Bay Area.

Michael Martin, vice president of Academic Services, was a voice of reason and an even-tempered counselor throughout the entire process. Mike was the seminary's longest serving employee, having been with

Gateway more than thirty years at the time of the relocation. He was a barometer revealing how the move impacted long-term employees and constituents. He was also a powerful example for them as he lived his conviction God had mandated this major change. Mike managed our academic programs, assured continued accreditation, solved problems the relocation caused for students related to completing their degrees, and maintained faculty morale. He also played a historic role in the final decision to pursue the relocation (recounted in chapter 3). Mike also inspired us with the passion for the seminary. He and his wife lived in a beautiful home in Northern California within a short distance of their two sons and their families. With only a few years until retirement, he gave up so much to move to Southern California. When asked about it, he said, "God called me to Gateway. God told the seminary to move. My only response is to start packing." His missional commitment was contagious.

Adam Groza, vice president of Enrollment and Student Services, was another important member of our team. Adam was a younger executive who had only been with the seminary a few years when the relocation was proposed. Throughout the discussions, Adam constantly advocated we think more about the future than the past, more about opportunities than obstacles. When we discussed fears about losing enrollment or potential negative impact on students, he argued instead for the improvements for students that would come from the reloca-tion. Adam was also an important conduit for information to students once the relocation was announced. Students trusted him because of his track record with them, and they rallied to support the relocation largely because of his efforts. Adam also took on a forerunner role, moving his family to Southern California and hiring a new enrollment team about a year before the seminary relocated. He worked from home, from the closest coffee shop, from a temporary office, and on airplanes flying back-and-forth between our old and new locations to facilitate

enrollment at both. He never let us forget that students—not buildings—are the essential ingredient of any seminary community.

Ben Skaug, vice president of advancement, was another younger
executive on our team. Ben came to work at the seminary while the
conflict over development options was raging. When he learned about
the situation during his interviews, he knew if we ever sold the campus
it would mean he would settle in Mill Valley just in time to relocate to
Ontario—and that's what happened. Within months after his family
arrived, the buyer approached us and the relocation became a reality.
Still learning his job in the old location, Ben was faced with creating a
new seminary in a new location. He was responsible for two key areas:
maintaining relationships with donors, and managing communications
about the relocation. His work with donors was stellar—contributions
increased during the relocation and we received several significant
gifts to facilitate it. He also did a remarkable job managing the initial
announcement and ongoing communication about the relocation. Like
Adam, Ben's family also moved to Southern California long before
the actual relocation. He created a new team, focused on launching
Gateway Seminary, and established key relationships among ministry
and community leaders. Ben made one other significant contribution—his relentless optimism and sense of humor helped keep us on an
even keel. God surprised us when he called Ben to a pastorate near the
Ontario campus soon after the move.

As Gary and Ben ended their service, two new men joined our
executive team. Tom Hixson became our vice president of business
services (overlapping with Gary for several months). Jeff Jones became
our vice president of advancement. Both of these men had a long history
with the seminary—Tom as a colleague in a partner ministry organization and Jeff as a former student and employee. Both jumped on the
speeding relocation train and made significant contributions during the
major change and transition. God called together a remarkable team of

colleagues and friends who shared a leadership experience that will bind us together for a lifetime.

God built our leadership team. He brought together men who had no idea they would someday move a seminary, and he enabled them to do so masterfully.

God Gave Us Special Gifts

God provided remarkable financial gifts during the relocation. In August 2016, just one month after closing the property sale, the seminary received an unsolicited $850,000 scholarship gift from a first-time donor. That just does not happen! This gift not only provided significant new scholarship funds, but also encouraged employees, trustees, and other constituents that relocation was the right decision. Since the seminary had received so much money from the property sale, some were concerned donors would stop supporting it. The opposite proved to be true. New donors joined the effort and some existing donors increased their gifts during the relocation.

In October 2016, Gateway received a $2.9 million land gift in Fremont, California where its new San Francisco Bay Area Campus is now located. A pastor read a press release about our search for property to build a regional, commuter-accessible campus in the Bay Area after we closed in Mill Valley. He discussed it with his leaders, secured approval from his church, and they donated about two acres of land perfectly situated for our needs. The seminary built its Fremont, California, campus on this site. This gift, like the scholarship previously described, was an unsolicited gift from a first-time donor—a church with a passion for shaping leaders who trusted Gateway to maximize the asset they provided us.

About a year later, we received a $500,000 gift to purchase a new missionary-in-residence home near the Ontario Campus. This gift also came in an unexpected way. When the seminary sold its former campus, its "missionary house" was included with the rest of the property.

We anticipated using some of the sale proceeds to replace it. A couple, however, learned of this opportunity and decided to make a special gift to buy a new house, furnish it, and provide a vehicle for missionaries to use while serving the seminary.

Besides these three major gifts, we also received many other special gifts for other relocation-related purposes. Overall donations increased during the relocation years as new friends stepped forward to confirm by their gifts the seminary was on the right track. Many existing donors inspired us by increasing their gifts, proving once again that people will give to fulfill a God-inspired and God-sized vision.

God gave us special gifts both to meet our needs and encourage us.

God Gave Us Governmental Favor

Part of the opposition we faced in Marin County came from governmental and political forces. In contrast, politicians and governmental leaders in both Ontario and Fremont embraced our mission, understood our time constraints, helped us resolve delaying snags, and welcomed us to their communities. In Ontario, we took the largest available free-standing office building off their tax role, and were granted permission to do so in a twelve-minute public hearing (without any opposition). In Fremont, we compacted a three-year process into one year. We did so without cutting corners, but with the cooperation of various city departments. In one meeting, a city employee listened to the complexities of our situation, pulled out a policy manual, and said, "Let's find some ways to streamline your process."

In the Bible, God's work is often attributed to or associated with secular leaders—kings, generals, and lesser rulers. Those stories took on new dimensions as the seminary experienced contemporary parallels. God uses governmental leaders to accomplish his purpose—sometimes prohibiting, sometimes permitting what he wants done. It really is true: "A king's heart is like channeled water in the LORD's hand: He directs it wherever he chooses" (Prov. 21:1).

God gave us governmental favor, helping us overcome obstacles and stay on his timetable.

God Enriched Us Financially

The financial results of the property sale and relocation have been amazing and humbling. The final sale price for the Mill Valley campus was $85 million, plus favorable terms for the two-year leaseback (including keeping all revenue generated on the campus). In addition, we received the $2.9 million land gift for the Fremont campus, the $850,000 scholarship gift, and the $500,000 gift for the missionary house in Ontario mentioned above. We were able to invest the liquid assets and use the real estate in favorable ways, which generated additional revenue. The $850,000 scholarship fund helped build enrollment, which increased income from tuition, fees, and housing rentals. The resources God provided strengthened us financially during the relocation. Plus, we still have the $4 million building lot that was included with the Ontario campus purchase.

We were able to purchase the Ontario building, complete the improvements transforming that building into a seminary campus, buy the two Ontario apartment complexes and the missionary house, and build the Fremont campus—all debt free—and still had about $30 million remaining (which has been invested as part of the seminary's endowment). When the projects were all completed, Gateway owned real estate valued at more than $70 million (all debt free) and had more than doubled its endowment!

God enriched us financially, providing long-term stability for pursuing his mission for the next generation.

God Gave Us Unity

Despite the awesome power shown in these first six miracles, perhaps the greatest demonstration of God's power during the relocation was the supernatural unity of the seminary community. We moved one of the largest seminaries in North America with minimal external opposition and no internal conflict. Our graduates supported us, most of our students stayed with us, and dozens of employees sacrificed to relocate with their colleagues.

God galvanized our employees, unifying faculty and staff in dramatic ways from the first announcement of the property sale. Our employees were aware of the conflict (it was hard to miss the protest signs and attacks in public hearings, not to mention their being accosted in grocery stores and at community events). This made them sensitive to the need for a resolution. When they heard my presentation regarding the campus sale, their response was measured and reflective. There were no emotional outbursts or angry explosions, only an overwhelming sense of the gravity and magnitude of the situation. Right after the announcement, our employees participated in dialogue sessions and processed the news carefully and prayerfully. They studied the information we provided and reflected on the reasons for the decision.

Two days later, the seminary community gathered for the first chapel service after the sale announcement. After some heart-felt comments from me praising the employees and students for their mature response to the relocation announcement, a senior faculty member stood up in the congregation and asked if he could speak. This was highly unusual during chapel, but his stature earned him the right to be heard. He said something close to this:

"Mr. President, I speak for myself, but I also think I speak for most of us here. We want you to know something. We are with you. You have made a courageous decision and it's the right decision. We are with you." The chapel erupted in a spontaneous standing ovation.

I stood there dumbfounded, thinking, "God, what is happening here? How is this even possible?" God was coalescing his people into a unified force expressed through that ovation. From that moment forward, while there was still much work needed to guide people through the transition (see chapter 4), there was never any doubt our employees and students would stand together to accomplish what seemed like an impossible challenge.

This same faculty member later posted a sign outside his office door that said, "The person who says something is impossible should not interrupt the person who is doing it."

Throughout the entire three-year process—from the sale announcement to being fully operational at our new campuses—we did not receive one letter, email, or visit from any employee expressing opposition to the relocation decision. While all struggled with the transition, they did so from a perspective of implementing the change, not opposing it.

The same unity was found among students. When we announced the relocation, our annual enrollment was just over two thousand students. Despite a huge surge of graduates who avoided relocating by finishing their degrees as fast as possible, new students kept enrolling (even during the two years they knew the seminary was moving) so that we still enrolled more than two thousand students the year we moved.

Our alumni, donors, trustees, and other constituents also stood unified with us. We received only one letter of opposition to the relocation decision—from an alum who later changed his mind once he had more information about the reasons for the sale. We received fewer than twenty critical emails—most of them one-liners from troubled people with messages like "Forgive them Father, they know not what they do" or "You are the devil!" With almost nine thousand graduates and countless thousands of other former students, the level of opposition was negligible. During planning for the sale announcement, we feared the worst and prepared to deal with a potential onslaught of negativity. It never materialized.

As a pastor in the Midwest, I had watched Golden Gate/Gateway from afar for many years. I read with great interest the news reports that the seminary was relocating—selling its primary campus and moving four hundred miles.

To my surprise, after the seminary had decided to move but prior to the actual location, I was elected as a trustee. Now I would get to see what was happening first hand. During new trustee orientation, I attended the first chapel at the new Ontario campus.

It was an overwhelming moment to be there as the opening song confessed the importance of the blood of Jesus. The joy on the faces of the faculty, staff, and students was heaven sent. They were not singing about leaving a campus, but about their mission. I stepped into the seminary community in the midst of victory and celebration of God's faithfulness. The unity was supernatural and the commitment to the seminary's mission evident everywhere. To God be the Glory!

Steve Davidson

Looking back, the primary reason for our unity—apart from God's grace poured out on us—was our seminary's shared commitment to our mission. Our mission is shaping leaders who expand God's kingdom around the world. Those are more than words for the Gateway family. We believe "the mission matters most," and we lived out that conviction in profound ways during the relocation.

God gave us unity. There's no explanation for it but his grace and his mission.

Was It Really a Miraculous Process?

Some people might read these stories and discount the claim the results were miraculous. After all, good leaders working with capable followers can do amazing things. Having lived through it, however, we know what happened is far beyond what anyone involved in the process could take credit for doing. There is only one reasonable explanation for how all these disparate circumstances came together. God intervened.

When it comes to leading major change, leaders show up for work every day and do their best. Followers make herculean efforts to support and implement major change—often sacrificing time, energy, and money for the cause. Those combined efforts, however, are not enough to produce supernatural outcomes. For major change to be successful, God must do what only he can do. For about three years, we experienced God in profound ways as he continually astounded us with his power. We were humbled by his sovereignty and awed by his omnipotence. We will never be the same for having lived through these remarkable experiences when God displayed his power in tangible ways among us.

9

Major Change Is Messy and Difficult

God leads people to make major changes for their good and his glory. God works miraculously to facilitate those changes. His direction and intervention do not, however, mean the process is orderly and tidy. The four major change stories describe in this book all eventually had good results—but not without significant difficulty along the way. These positive outcomes do not mean everything always went well, decisions were made without conflict, financial provision came easily, timetables dovetailed, and every deadline was met. The final results achieved the desired outcomes, but the pathway was often crooked, confusing, and convoluted.

During major change, there are days when both leaders and followers wonder, "What were we thinking?" and more seriously, "Did we miss God's leading?" The challenges can be formidable and discouraging. Reaching the destination successfully does not mean the journey was easy, but when major change is accomplished, it is common to look back and celebrate the successes and minimize the difficulties. Hindsight has a purifying and insulating effect—like women who give birth and later decide to have additional children. The pain of the birth recedes as the joy of parenting makes the travail worthwhile. So it is with major change. The process is messy and difficult, but worth it in the long run.

After the land sale announcement, I was the first employee hired during the transition. We moved from the Midwest to a rental house in the Ontario area and lived on a single income for six months. At that point, my wife also took a job with the seminary. For about two years we lived and worked in a rented condo, were four hundred miles from most other seminary employees, did almost all our work electronically, and tried to learn new jobs having never worked before for any school.

Then, a whole new set of changes came our way. The seminary finally moved, we bought a house near the new campus, and we started learning how to work in an office with daily staff interaction. While all that was going on, we were also trying to find a church. While we visited many good churches, we had a sense God had something else for us to do. Six months after the seminary opened in Ontario, we teamed up with some other employees and students to start a new church.

We have lived through constant change, some turmoil, and a huge amount of starting-over for people at a stage in life when settling down is usually the goal. We did it all for one simple reason: the mission matters most.

Jay and Becky Badry

Reality at Jericho

The Jericho story underscores the harsh reality of how chaotic major change can be. Joshua conquering Jericho is often told as a heartwarming story of obedience and God's miraculous power—sometimes even reduced to a cute Bible story for children. While it illustrates obedience and power, it does so while reporting the ruthless annihilation of a city—humans, animals, and material all obliterated. a scorched earth policy of total war.

When God directed Joshua to conquer Jericho, he gave specific instructions to the Israelites about their role in the attack. They were to march around the city once a day for six days, then make seven laps on the seventh day. At the end of the final trip around the city, Joshua told them:

> "Shout! For the LORD has given you the city. But the city and everything in it are set apart to the LORD for destruction. Only Rahab the prostitute and everyone with her in the house will live, because she hid the messengers we sent. But keep yourselves from the things set apart, or you will be set apart for destruction. If you take any of those things, you will set apart the camp of Israel for destruction and make trouble for it. For all the silver and gold, the articles of bronze and iron, are dedicated to the LORD and must go into the LORD's treasury." So the troops shouted, and the trumpets sounded. When they heard the blast of the trumpet, the troops gave a great shout, and the wall collapsed. The troops advanced into the city, each man straight ahead, and they captured the city. They completely destroyed everything in the city with the sword—every man and woman, both young and old, and every ox, sheep, and donkey." (Josh. 6:16b–21)

When the conquest was over, "they burned the city and everything in it, but they put the silver and gold and the articles of bronze and iron into the treasury of the LORD's house" (Josh. 6:24).

The gory aspects of the story must not be minimized. God ordered a slaughter and his people fulfilled his mandate. Major change at Jericho meant intense conflict, destruction of property, and loss of life amidst a chaotic attack. Menacing soldiers killed innocent children and defenseless animals. Families were wiped out. Possessions were burned. Messy and difficult are significant understatements of what happened at Jericho.

Conflict Comes with Change

While major ministry changes today do not involve anything like this level of violence, they do often include significant conflicts which make them challenging in their own way. Change is hard and major change doubly so. Managing the conflicts associated with major change is a significant problem for leaders who are also going through the change, dealing with personal emotional and spiritual issues while trying to lead the organization, as well as helping their followers process the transition. For all these reasons, managing major change and the accompanying conflicts is challenging.

Learning to diagnose and respond to conflict associated with major change is a significant skill for ministry leaders. Some resources for this are readily available: biblical precedents, practical books, and conflict management seminars. Unfortunately, while all these are helpful, learning to handle conflict well requires field training. Leaders must live through some conflict, likely making some mistakes in dealing with it, as part of learning how to manage it well. Relational battle scars are both an occupational hazard and experiential necessity for mastering this difficult area of ministry leadership.

Part of learning to handle conflict well is recognizing the difference between healthy and unhealthy conflict. Some conflict can actually be a positive aspect of adopting major change. Discerning the difference between healthy conflict (and encouraging it) and unhealthy conflict (and ministering effectively through it) is a vital skill for leaders. Doing this poorly exacerbates the conflict and leads to further division and loss of missional momentum. Doing it well turns conflict into a disciple-making tool for personal and organizational growth.

Encouraging Healthy Conflict

Relational conflict can occur in at least three interpersonal dimensions: struggles with God, debates among decision-makers, and tensions among followers as they process the change they are attempting to make. While these can be negative, each can also be a source of healthy conflict contributing to making major change.

Struggles with God

Deciding to lead a major change involves wrestling with God to determine his will about the change, the timetable for the change, and methodology for implementing the change. These decisions are not easy. Leaders endure profound spiritual struggles trying to discern God's direction about a major change. These are ministry-making, career-breaking decisions which set the course of a church or organization for a generation. Discovering God's plan is essential before undertaking any such endeavor.

Making the final decision to relocate the seminary was difficult. Many long nights of prayer, punctuated by significant anxiety and worry, were part of making the decision. There was no one defining decision-moment—just a long, slow slog until clarity dawned as a result of personal devotion, professional consideration, and debate-filled dialogue. The decision took its toll mentally, spiritually, and physically.

Sometime later, hindsight about this produced a humorous teaching moment. After recounting this struggle for employees and students, I told them, "My new life verse is 'Be anxious about everything.' I lived it out perfectly!" An employee created a screensaver which has my "verse" and the reference "Hesitations 4:6a." We had a good laugh then, but it was no laughing matter when the struggle was happening.

Ministry leaders love their followers and know they have to "get it right" on the big decisions. Those decisions are not always easy; God's direction is sometimes hard to discern. God is not elusive, but our egos and sinful imperfection make sorting out his spiritual direction difficult. Good leaders are resolute, however, in wrestling with God (and themselves) until they have the clarity they need. It is a price leaders pay before leading others into major changes with such profound implications.

Debates among Decision-makers

Healthy debate among people charged with leading major change is part of a good decision-making process. When necessary, wise leaders even encourage appropriate conflict to make sure all issues are aired and all aspects of a complicated decision are put on the table. Most of the time, leadership teams are composed of strong-willed people who speak their mind (that is one reason they are on the team). Senior leaders, who ride herd on these groups, must know when to spur them on and when to rein them in to facilitate the best decision possible.

The seminary's executive team participated in countless hours of protracted meetings trying to decide the relocation issue. Those discussions started in 2009, when we first had to propose a solution to the expiring master plan. We concluded we should remain at the Mill Valley location and pursue redevelopment of the campus. That decision was not made easily or flippantly. We engaged in prolonged discussions for months before coming to that conclusion. While the seminary ultimately relocated instead, I still believe redevelopment was the right decision at that time. Neither the seminary community, the leadership team, nor the board were ready to sell the campus and relocate. Our unity about developing the property was part of God keeping us on his timetable for the real major change only he knew was coming.

Later, this same team was faced with the challenge of reconsidering our options and making the decision to relocate. Again, we had multiple meetings over many months (the entire process lasted five years). Those were often intense meetings—with tables pounded and voices raised. We fought like brothers—going at it tooth and toenail in private, but always standing together in public. When we finally reached a unified decision to recommend relocation, it was a solid decision, thoroughly vetted with no stone unturned and no opposition left unspoken. The conflicts among us, expressed through robust debate, enabled us to make the right decision at the right time.

Our board engaged in similar discussions, with the advantage of having the results and summary of our leadership team debates (and the information they produced) before them. This shortened their discussions, but did not make them less intense. One of the most profound moments in the decision-making process was when the board went into executive session (no staff present) and reached the final decisions about relocating and rebranding the seminary. Board members later described this session as sober and intense. When that session was over, they voted on the issues by secret, written ballot—and the votes were unanimous on every recommendation. When the chairman reported the vote, he said, "These are our decisions and we will not waver. Whatever happens, Dr. Iorg, we will stand with you. We have made this decision together and we will stand together." And stand they did, never wavering after making one of the most significant board decisions in seminary history. Robust, honest, forthright debate contributed to the confidence the board had in its final decisions.

It was a much less formal process when the church in Missouri decided to move, but no less intense. The first proposal to consider relocating the church was derided and rejected by the church's deacons (the leadership body at the time). About two years later, after trying various alternatives to creating more space, the idea of moving was again broached. This time, the deacons were more amenable. The senior deacon who had previously opposed the idea made the motion to form the study committee to investigate land options. The internal debate over the previous months—both formally in the meetings and informally over coffee—had reshaped his thinking. Once the deacons and pastors were unified, the idea of relocating gained credibility with the church. The study committee was formed; the land at the new location became available, and the church ultimately moved.

Conflict among leaders trying to decide about a major change can be a healthy part of the process when it engenders honest debate. As long as the debate remains focused on core issues, it will lead to greater insight and unity about the final decision. But when any debate becomes personal—more focused on winners and losers than advancing the organization's mission—it becomes detrimental. The spiritual maturity and missional focus of ministry leaders should keep the debate appropriately centered. When it drifts, team members have to take corrective action to get it back on track. Otherwise, what could be a force for good can poison the decision-making process.

Tension among Followers

When major change is announced, followers often feel anxious. They may be troubled about the decision itself, questioning if it is the right one for the church or organization. They may also be unsettled because of what they fear the change may mean for them. They have questions like, "What does this mean for me? Do I still have a job? How much will I be expected to give? How will this change impact my family?" Tension resulting from these questions is a natural response among followers when they first learn about a major change, feel the sense of loss it produces, and consider its implications for them.

Tension among followers facing change is different than dissension about the change or open resistance to the change. Those responses will be considered later in this chapter. Some leaders make the mistake of lumping all these together and responding to them in a similar fashion. Tension resulting from honest questions or personal concerns about a proposed change demands a different response than dissension or opposition.

Tension among followers can be alleviated by three strategies. First, provide information that answers the questions followers have about the change. Second, allow adequate time for followers to process that information and consider the implications of the change. Third, as a leader, give your followers permission to dialogue about their concerns—with you, with other leaders, and with each other.

This concept was outlined earlier, along with an excerpt from a presentation to the seminary community (see chapter 4). It bears repeating because of the importance of leaders facilitating dialogue among followers to aid with transition:

We have also been frank about the impact transition is having on all of us. Remember, change is the new set of circumstances but transition is our response to them. The best model to understand that response is the "grief process" model. We have used the six-phase grief model of shock, anger, denial, bargaining, exploration, and adjustment. I have repeatedly reviewed this model with you. I have encouraged you to be honest about your feelings as you move through these phases. Talking to your fellow employees or fellow students about what you are going through is an essential part of working through the transition.

Let me underscore this. Honest dialogue—including shedding tears and venting frustrations—is essential to working through grief and reaching the "adjustment" phase. When you talk about these issues, you are not being rebellious, murmuring, gossiping, undermining my leadership, or being disloyal to our mission. You are being a normal Christian grappling with what God is doing with all of us.

Sometimes, Christian leaders demonize followers who don't immediately embrace change announced to them. They are labeled "rebels" or called "divisive." We will not do that here. We recognize change is hard and transition is the process every person goes through to assimilate it. I would rather have you express your feelings and work through them, than fake agreement for fear you will be shamed for showing spiritual transparency.

Earlier, I lauded our unity over the past months. We are experiencing unity—real unity, not the fake kind. Real unity means we share a bedrock commitment to our mission. It doesn't mean everyone agrees with every decision being made, every policy being implemented, or every personnel choice. It doesn't mean we don't feel shock, anger, denial, and would like to bargain ways to make the whole situation easier. Real unity means we are more committed to our mission than our personal comfort. Real unity only comes when people have the freedom to work through a process to get there.

By recognizing the need to process the transition in community, we created space for employees and students to share their feelings, talk about their options, draw strength from one another, and pray together. We recognized the difference between tension surrounding the transition and dissension about or opposition to the change. We accepted tension as a normal part of the process. We refused to demonize those who expressed their pain and experienced the power of genuine unity as people came together to support the relocation effort.

In 2012, the company where I had worked for fifteen years made massive cuts and I was terminated. It was devastating. I took another IT job at a mega-corporation, but was still unfulfilled.

My pastor told me about Gateway moving to our area. I applied to be the Director of Information Technology and was soon hired. It has been a perfect fit for me—a smaller organization where my daily leadership can make a difference and God's mission is advanced.

Soon after I was hired—right in the middle of the relocation, during an all-hands meeting—we were encouraged to break up in small groups for prayer. This was inconceivable to me—praying at work with my colleagues! Our leaders did many other things to show support for us and to help us support each other.

God truly is "able to do above and beyond all that we ask or think according to the power that works in us" (Eph. 3:20). He did more than answer my prayers for a job; he gave me a place to use my professional skills, work with people who care about each other, and further the message of Christ.

Steve Polcyn

Ministering Effectively during Unhealthy Conflict

While healthy conflict is a positive part of leading major change, unhealthy conflict can also be part of the equation. There are two primary sources of unhealthy conflict, and both must be confronted and handled appropriately to keep them from derailing the fulfillment of a major change. The first source comes from inside the organization; the other from outside.

Dissent from Insiders

When a major change is announced, some followers may oppose the decision and attempt to undermine the process. Their conflict is not tension about the transition; it is opposition to the change. Their goal is to stop the major change from happening. Sometimes, the opposition comes from surprising sources and is based on interesting reasons.

When the Missouri church decided to move, one person said in a public meeting, "I have walked the property, and the ground won't hold up a church building. It's porous and we will never be able to build on it." This surprising conclusion was from a person who had previously been a strong supporter of almost everything the church did. Despite assurances to the contrary (including an engineering study), he never changed his mind about the quality of the land. He and his wife voted against the relocation (the only two no votes when the final decision was made).

When the new vision for the convention was presented, an older pastor spoke against it. He referenced a "blue bridge" most people had driven over to attend the meeting and called for additional "guardrails" to be added to the proposal to prevent the convention "veering off course" in the future. His opposition was based on fears of lost identity and changes to long-established practices he appreciated. It was painful to hear such a veteran leader voice those concerns and even more painful to watch when his motion was decisively defeated.

While the followers in these examples opposed those changes, they did not continue to resist them after the final decisions were made. They were cooperative members who voiced their perspective, voted their convictions, and then moved on with the majority. Whether the final decision is made by a board in an organization, messengers or delegates at a convention, elders in some churches, or the congregation in others, some normally supportive followers may oppose the change. This does not necessarily equal divisive dissent, depending on their actions after the decision is finalized. If they acquiesce to the decision, they can continue as non-adopters who enjoy the fruit of the change without making much effort to support it. If, on the other hand, they continue to aggressively oppose the adopted change, they have to leave the church or organization.

Leaders cannot allow major change to be jeopardized by persistent attacks undermining its implementation. Since it is a major change, implementation will consume the energies of the leaders. They cannot dissipate their efforts by continuing to manage persistent critics. Church members may have to be removed, employees terminated, or board members replaced. Since major change determines the future of a ministry, no matter how painful it may be, people who threaten accomplishment of the change may have to leave for the long-term well being of the organization.

Attack from Outsiders

Some major change invites conflict with people and entities outside the ministry organization. When the seminary attempted to develop its former campus, we faced significant opposition from political leaders, governmental workers, community organizers, and aggressive individuals. We were personally threatened and publicly picketed. Our opponents employed land use consultants and attorneys in a concerted effort to limit our future options. Dealing with all this was onerous and draining.

The chief responsibilities for ministry leaders related to attacks from outside their organizations are two-fold. First, protect the ministry organization. Corporations, which most churches and ministries are, have legal rights and privileges that must be protected. It is within the ethical and moral purview of Christian leaders to use every legitimate means to enforce those rights. Second, minimize the influence of detractors on daily operations. Some leaders mistakenly focus too much public attention on their detractors. For about four months, protestors held up a huge banner at the entrances to several of our campuses condemning my leadership. The banner said: "Shame on Jeff Iorg" and included a seminary phone number to call and complain about me. While hundreds of people saw these displays daily, my comments about them were very limited. While leaders can acknowledge outside attackers, they should minimize, rather than magnify, their influence. Do not make them agenda items in meetings, fodder for social media posts, subjects of sermons, or topics for hallway conversations.

Principles for Managing Conflict

Accepting the reality of conflict associated with major changes in churches and ministry organizations may seem like settling for a substandard version of Christian leadership. It is not. Facing reality should never be equated with compromising standards. Conflict in Christian ministry is not new. It occurred frequently (and was usually managed well) in New Testament churches and among prominent New Testament-era leaders. Wise leaders spend less time decrying conflict as unspiritual or unnecessary and more time developing a principled response for managing it in their ministry setting. Teaching the following principles and following them as normal leadership practices will help leaders minister more effectively during conflict related to major change.

Anticipate Conflict

Wise leaders anticipate conflict. They know it has been part of ministry leadership since the founding of the church.

The early church experienced conflict among its members (Phil. 4:2–3a). Two women—Euodia and Syntyche—were urged to "agree in the Lord." Paul described them as "women who have contended for the gospel at my side," meaning they were mature Christians. Yet, their conflict was so serious Paul addressed it in an open church letter.

The early church also experienced conflict over personnel. (Acts 15:36–41) John Mark had abandoned Paul and Barnabas on an earlier mission trip. Now, as they prepared for another trip, "Barnabas wanted to take along John Mark. But Paul insisted that they should not take along this man who had deserted them." The conflict between Paul and Barnabas was embittering and divisive, ending when there was "such a sharp disagreement that they parted company." It forced other leaders to choose sides as "Paul chose Silas and departed" separately from Barnabas and Mark. There is also some indication the Antioch church was disrupted as they had to choose which team to support, sending Paul and Silas off "after being commended by the brothers and sisters to the grace of the Lord" (with no mention of support for Barnabas and Mark).

There was also conflict between prominent church leaders. Peter and Paul got into a dispute over table fellowship with Gentiles. Paul described the conflict when he wrote, "I opposed him (Peter) to his face . . . in front of everyone" (Gal. 2:11, 14). That must have been quite a showdown—two spiritual heavyweights arguing faith and practice in a public dispute!

The early church also had conflict over doctrine—like the dispute over circumcision and the nature of the gospel (Acts 15:1–35). When the conflict erupted, Paul and Barnabas "engaged them in serious argument and debate." The debate, its intensity, and its resolution take up an entire chapter in the early church's history recorded in Acts. This underscores the importance of this story as a model for handling theological conflict.

The early church had conflict between members, conflict about personnel, conflict between prominent leaders, and conflict over fundamental doctrinal questions—just to name a few examples. If the nascent church had these problems, why should leaders today expect the contemporary church to be any better? Two thousand years of church history mandates a different conclusion—the church has always had and will always have internal conflicts.

Wise leaders anticipate this and are proactive in preparing for conflict. Preparation for conflict includes preaching or teaching on it as a routine part of organizational development, studying conflict management with a leadership team, and minimizing anticipated conflict as soon as it appears on the horizon. Being proactive means taking steps to inform and educate people about conflict before it happens, not reactively waiting until it happens. It also means solving small problems before they become large ones—preventing little fires from raging out of control and causing irreparable damage.

Address Conflict Intentionally

While no one really likes facing up to conflict, wise leaders know they must take initiative to deal with it. It seldom goes away on its own. Dealing with conflict requires leaders to go where angels fear to tread.

Addressing conflict within an organization requires dealing directly with opponents (and/or helping them face each other). Meeting with people who oppose leadership decisions about major change is difficult. Yet adequately resolving those issues requires personal interaction. Despite the prevalence of electronic media, these conversations and meetings are best done face-to-face. Body language, vocal tones, and other non-verbal nuances make all the difference in determining the true meaning behind the words used to communicate about delicate matters. It is easier to discern true issues driving a conflict and ferret out extraneous information clouding their judgment by having personal meetings with troubled followers. Another advantage of these meetings is the opportunity to pray together, even kneeling together or otherwise demonstrating mutual submission to God while seeking a resolution.

The most challenging part of facing conflict intentionally is discerning when productive dialogue is over and the decision to end a relationship has to be made. Pastoral leaders dread those conversations. We are shepherds who collect and protect a flock, not divide and drive away sheep. When it becomes evident unity about a major change is not possible, there are only two options left for disaffected followers: quiet cooperation with the new direction or separation from the organization. Allowing them to remain in open conflict hampers the mission, and therefore, is not an option. Reach this conclusion slowly and carefully, but have the courage to make those decisions when absolutely necessary.

One mistake leaders make when addressing conflict is responding disproportionally to the level of the opposition expressed. In other words, do not make more of the conflict than it really is. Just because a person posts a critical comment or a snarky question on Facebook does not mandate convening an elders meeting to discuss church discipline. Make sure your plan for addressing detractors is in proportion to the seriousness of the opposition to accomplishing the major change (and therefore, the organization's mission), not just a response to your wounded pride or hurt feelings.

Another common mistake is addressing conflict in a public forum—like preaching about it, mentioning it in a blog, or discussing it in a hallway conversation. Doing so is cowardly and deceitful. If a conflict needs to be addressed with a person or a group, meet with them directly and intentionally. Do not use public forums to solve interpersonal issues—even when the attacks may come through a public forum. Leaders cannot control comments from detractors, but they can control their response. Leaders must choose wisely how, when, and where to interact with people in conflict with major change decisions.

Resolve Conflict Appropriately

When leaders resolve conflict appropriately, they reach the best decision possible—not necessarily one that makes everyone happy. The goal of conflict resolution—particularly conflict related to major change—is advancing the organization's mission as it aligns with God's mission. When leaders resolve conflict with a leadership decision, the goal is not compromising to accommodate a mitigated version of the proposed change. Rather, the goal is advancing the mission by implementing the major change successfully. The focus of the resolution process is helping everyone understand how the major change is related to the mission and how they must adjust their expectations accordingly.

There are two possible healthy outcomes for conflict resolution about major change related to organizational mission. First, leaders and followers agree to work together to implement the change and accomplish their shared mission. Second, leaders and followers agree to separate and continue to advance God's mission, but in a different church or ministry, with people who have a different organizational mission. Those are the only two acceptable options.

There are two other options—both unacceptable. First, it is untenable for leaders and followers who cannot agree on a major change to remain together. Christians share different convictions about many optional aspects of church ministry and organizational function. Life is too short for prolonged arguments over these issues. Time is better spent moving on from conflicted relationships and finding a church or ministry with a compatible vision.

A second unacceptable option is using conflict as an excuse for dropping out of Christian service. That is never an option! Conflict may be a signal to move to a different church or organization, but never an excuse to abandon God's mission. When believers do this, they are using conflict to validate their pride. A far better choice is moving to another setting more aligned with their convictions about the mission, method, and practice of ministry.

Accept Mixed Outcomes

Part of resolving conflict well in organizations is learning to accept mixed outcomes. When a conflict is successfully resolved—particularly in a large organization—some people will be pleased, others will be disappointed, some will stay fully engaged, and some will leave for other opportunities. Most leaders want every conflict to end with everyone happy and satisfied, but that is seldom the case.

Another aspect of accepting mixed outcomes is not personalizing the results of conflict resolution. When leaders make a good faith effort and do their best to resolve a conflict, anything less than total unity can feel like failure. The emotional and spiritual responses of other people, however, are too heavy a burden to place on any leader. Good leaders sometimes feel like failures when people withdraw their support or leave their church or ministry. Wise leaders manage those feelings, recognizing them but not legitimizing them as the final barometer on their conflict resolution effectiveness. Leaders who cannot accept mixed results are doomed to a perpetual sense of frustration with themselves and the people they lead.

Move On

Once every effort has been made to resolve a conflict, regardless of the result, leaders must move on. Stop revisiting, talking about, and thinking about the conflict. Move on! Easier said than done, right?

The key to moving on from unsatisfactory conflict resolution is refocusing on accomplishing your mission. Do this by proactively implementing the major change. Make a list of what needs to be done to accomplish your mission. Then, get started on it. Filling your time with meaningful, purposeful activity is the best antidote for the malaise felt after trying unsuccessfully to resolve stubborn conflict. Proactive effort reshapes thinking and eliminates wasted hours mulling over the vagaries of less-than-perfect conflict resolution.

When it comes to managing conflict, do the best you can. Make an honest, prayerful effort, and move on. God has called leaders to minister effectively during conflict, not resolve it perfectly every time. He has commissioned leaders to advance his mission by carrying out the mission of their church or ministry organization. When every reasonable and spiritual effort to resolve conflict has been exhausted, avoid perpetual preoccupation with the past at the expense of missional advance. It's time to move on.

10

Major Change
Glorifies God

When major change is done well by God's standards, God is glorified. That is the ultimate goal of every ministry leader, as theologians have concluded for centuries and millions of catechized children can recite: "Man's chief end is to glorify God, and to enjoy him forever."[17]

Completing a major change is often perceived as the primary goal, but the ultimate goal of all Christian service is glorifying God. Paul taught the same principle when he advocated, "So, whether you eat or drink, or whatever you do, do everything for the glory of God" (1 Cor. 10:31). God's work done God's way magnifies his name and brings him greater fame.

Conquering for God's Glory

When Joshua led the conquest of Jericho, the battle-plan originated with God, was empowered by God, resulted in riches being collected for God, and brought glory to God. Joshua told the people, "Shout! For the LORD has given you the city" (Josh. 6:16) and "the city and everything in it are set apart to the LORD for destruction" (Josh. 6:17). He also warned the army to, "keep yourselves from the things set apart, or you will be set apart for destruction. If you take any of those things, you will set apart the camp of Israel for destruction and make trouble for it. For all the silver and gold, and the articles of bronze and iron, are dedicated to the LORD and must go into the LORD's treasury" (Josh. 6:18–19). While Joshua had courageously stepped forward to lead and his followers were prepared to fight the battle, they all understood God was the originator and sustainer of their plans. Moreover, Joshua's warning was clear. The seriousness of the need for obedience was revealed by what happened after the battle of Jericho ended.

Joshua and his army moved to the next conquest, the city of Ai. Scouts were sent to ascertain the enemy's strength and plot the means to overtake that stronghold (Josh. 7:1–4). They attacked with what they assumed would be sufficient forces for victory. The Israelites, however, were routed. They fled in panic and Joshua cried out to God for answers (Josh. 7:5–9). God responded and told Joshua, "Stand up! Why have you fallen face-down? Israel has sinned. They have violated My covenant that I appointed for them. They have taken some of what was set apart. They have stolen, deceived, and put those things with their own belongings" (Josh. 7:10–11). He then gave Joshua instructions for isolating the disobedient individuals responsible for the theft (Josh. 7:13–15). Joshua followed through and Achan and his clan were identified. When outed, Achan said, "It is true. I have sinned against the LORD, the God of Israel. This is what I did: When I saw among the spoils a beautiful cloak from Babylon, five pounds of silver, and a bar of gold weighing a pound and a quarter, I coveted them and took them. You can see for yourself. They are concealed in the ground inside my tent, with the silver under the cloak" (Josh. 7:20–21).

Achan's sin was costly for him, his family, and the nation as a whole. The Israelites lost the battle of Ai as soldiers died, the nation was humiliated, and confidence was diminished. Achan's family was punished severely for their sin and the resulting debacle as "all Israel stoned them to death. They burned their bodies, threw stones on them, and raised over him a large pile of rocks that remains still today" (Josh. 7:25b–26). This message is clear: God will not share his glory nor allow disobedience to mar the purity of service done in his name.

God's work done God's way resounds to his glory. His name is placed on the marquee. His name is put up in lights. God takes center stage as the star of the show. In the end, people walk away talking more about God than anyone on the program.

Because we want this to be true, we wonder, "How then do we glorify God?" "What can we do to glorify him through major change?" While the outcome might seem elusive, the steps to facilitate the process are practical and doable.

Do Work Worthy of God's Name

God is glorified when a major change is worthy of being done in his name. Grand projects that require sacrificial effort and result in people becoming Christians, churches being started or enlarged, human needs being met, or holy causes advanced are worthy of God's name. Athletes who compete for their country in international events are inspired to play for the name on the front of the jersey, not their name on the back. They give superhuman effort, often without being paid, because the cause and the result are worthy of selfless effort. In a similar but more profound way, whatever we do in God's name must have the same attention to detail, unselfish motivation, and demonstrable passion.

Christians do ministry—including making major changes—to fulfill God's mission, enhance his reputation, and expand awareness of God's activity in the world. What is done in God's name requires the best effort that can be given, the most generous allocation of resources possible, and an intentional commitment to excellence.

Doing ministry with excellence means doing the best we can with what we have. Excellence is always defined situationally. When Gateway Seminary hosts a presidential event, they are done as nicely as our resources allow. When the president of the United States hosts a state dinner, excellence in that setting exceeds anything the seminary can do. Excellence is always relative and determined contextually. An economically challenged church in a poor community can still do ministry with excellence—as long as they do all they can with what they have, giving their selfless best in God's name.

Another aspect of determining excellence—particularly when making major change—is allocating resources wisely. Those decisions must be mission-driven, not just made to please leaders or pacify followers. When a major change involves constructing facilities, for example, it is challenging to hit the sweet spot between functional and lavish. People want to be proud of what is built, but not embarrassed by resources wasted on luxuries. The goal of new facilities—as with all major changes—is advancing God's mission, not meeting the ego needs of leaders or making followers more comfortable. Excellence means accomplishing God's mission of gathering people for his eternal companionship, not trying to impress God by what we build for him.

There is wide latitude in determining God's best in every major change situation. People naturally see issues from their perspective, colored by their background, expectations, and resources. It is challenging to strike a balance between extravagance and frugality, mission and maintenance, and the needs of current and future constituents. As leaders strategize major change, the mission (both God's and the ministry's) must be a primary guide in shaping those decisions. When disciplined decision-making processes are applied, reasonable choices will result in positive outcomes. God's mission will be accomplished, and he will be glorified by the quality of work done in his name.

Magnify God's Role in Your Success

Another way to glorify God is to magnify his role in any success achieved through a major change. The Bible says, "Ascribe to the LORD glory and strength" and "Ascribe to the LORD the glory due his name" (Ps. 29:1–2). Another way to say this is "give God the credit" for whatever happens. Ministry leaders must practice the discipline of graciously accepting compliments but ascribing glory to God for every success. Otherwise, kind words become poisonous, puffing up egos and convincing leaders their superior abilities (with God's occasional help, of course) are the source of their success.

When a church or ministry accomplishes something significant, both the leaders and followers may naturally achieve greater notoriety. For example, multiple organizations have asked members of our executive team to help them with issues related to major change because of our experience moving the seminary. These are natural opportunities to share what has been learned, but also tantalizing temptations to overstate our role in what happened. While leaders should share best practices and learning moments from their experiences, Christian leaders must not insinuate their skills were satisfactory for spiritual achievements. Only God can do those things—and leaders must give him glory.

Many good decisions by leaders and effective actions by followers are part of any successful major change. While those actions are significant, magnifying God's role in accomplishing those major changes is much more important. Leaders do this by emphasizing God's role when telling their story. The most enjoyable part of writing this book was retelling the story of the seven miracles (see chapter 8). God intervened in relocating and inaugurating Gateway Seminary. His work surpassed anything anyone else did in the process. We give him glory!

The same thing could be written about the other major change stories illustrating the principles in this book. Give God glory! He provided land for a church in Missouri; he provided land and finances for a church campus in Oregon; he unified a diverse convention around a new ministry paradigm (including new facilities); and he provided a buyer for distressed land no one thought could ever be sold—along with everything else needed to relocate a seminary. God did what only he could do. Give him glory!

Besides telling the corporate story of God's intervention, another way to give God glory is facilitating members, employees, and constituents in telling personal stories of God's work through them during a major change. Some of the most moving stories in the context of major change are the stories of individuals who experienced God's miraculous intervention making their participation possible. Publicize those stories. Encourage people to tell them in worship services, in planning meetings, through social media, and on blogs.

I was one of those for whom the seminary's move hit hardest. I had served on the faculty since 1986, meaning my life's work was the cumulative impact of our school.

But with whole-hearted commitment and interest, I joined the process of making the seminary's move all it could and should be for God's kingdom and future generations of seminarians. I rejoiced at the stories of God's hand moving at critical junctures in the process. I rejoiced at the regular reports of God's goodness and guidance and in the many out-workings of his providence—both small and large—people were experiencing in the move. I was surprised, however, when I became the recipient of an undeniable sign of God's grace.

I had not rented a home in decades, so my wife and I were surprised to find, after spending two days looking for a suitable rental, we had to bid on properties much like when buying a property. We were outbid on our first attempts and were, understandably, disappointed. Weeks later we found another property and entered the negotiations somewhat chastened and uncertain. When we asked what we would need to do to secure the property, the word came back: "Well, you don't have to worry about that. My wife is a graduate of Golden Gate and we would like you to be there." We felt the tangible touch of God's providence and presence as he went before us and lined up rental property near our new campus owned by someone trained as part of our past efforts.

God worked like this to solve practical needs for dozens of families. We give him glory for his faithfulness and goodness!

John Shouse

When Gateway relocated, dozens of employees experienced God's provision of new jobs for spouses, new schools for children, and new houses for families. They were also awed by coordination of circumstances related to financial support, extended family obligations, and professional opportunities—all so complex only God could have put the pieces together. When these stories are shared, God is glorified. When people feel overwhelmed, knowing their situation is beyond their control, and are then delivered in unimaginable ways, they give God glory. They magnify his name spontaneously, fervently, and without inhibition—hands are raised, tears are shed, shouts are heard, and amens are voiced. People know their limitations and recognize God's activity when they see it. They readily give him glory by telling their stories. Many of them are sprinkled throughout this book as examples of God's power demonstrated in dozens of different situations.

Celebrate Obedience and Sacrifice

A common theme among followers who accomplish a major change is obedient sacrifice. Their stories glorify God because they communicate the high value they place on their relationship with him. One family gave a large stock fund they had accumulated for over thirty years to construct the church in Oregon. They gave the gift because of their all-out commitment to God's mission expressed through a church they believed was aligned with that mission. A widow gave the first gift to help purchase the land for the Missouri church—$500. She sacrificed to make this gift because she wanted a strong church to, in her words, "reach the next generation for the Lord." When the convention adopted its new ministry paradigm, a staff member said, "I will give the rest of my ministry life to accomplishing this vision." He then expended fifteen productive years of ministry service—sacrificing time, energy, and money—to advance God's kingdom by helping start dozens of new churches. These stories illustrate obedience to and sacrifice for God.

They also raise the question, "what constitutes a sacrifice?" in the context of accomplishing a major change today.

Sacrifice Is Personal

It is impossible for anyone to define what constitutes a sacrifice for someone else. No one really knows the motives, desires, impulses, or secret longings of another person. No one else understands the emotional investment in what a person is surrendering, the events and circumstances triggering those connections, and their strength of faith required in that moment. What might appear to be a great sacrifice to one person, another person might not consider all that difficult. In other cases, what others might consider insignificant may create emotional turmoil and spiritual angst for someone else.

When we moved the seminary, leaving behind personal ministry commitments and church-based relationships was the hardest sacrifice for many people. Since their seminary community was moving with them, the greatest relational loss was giving up long-established connections in churches and ministries. Those sacrifices produced some of the most emotional moments in the relocation.

Another significant sacrifice for many was giving up living in the Bay Area—a unique place marked by geographic beauty, cultural opportunities, fabulous restaurants, diverse neighborhoods, and spiritual challenges many found invigorating. While some outsiders thought moving from that bastion of secularism would be a relief, many seminary personnel felt they were abandoning front-line responsibility for representing God in one of the most spiritually challenged places in North America. While being there might have appeared to outsiders to be a sacrifice, those who actually lived there found leaving more painful than staying.

God must have an amazing sense of humor. I accepted a position at Golden Gate and moved from the desert in Phoenix. I never considered teaching in the Los Angeles area—it is too crowded and the traffic is terrible. We moved to Mill Valley, got comfortable in the Bay Area, gained new friends, joined a great church, and found new doctors and dentists.

Then God told our seminary to move. I could see God's hand working in moving the school, but that does not mean it was easy for us. The only reason we put ourselves through another move was for God's plan and glory to be accomplished. It was never about our ease or happiness. God never promised us those things. His plans must always take precedence over our desires.

Most days, that's really easy to remember. But some days are harder—like when I really miss the ocean. I had never lived by the ocean before and did not expect moving away from it to be an issue. Some days though, I just miss it and think about what we gave up to move to a place we never would have chosen under other circumstances.

Paul Wegner

Sacrifice is intensely personal. While leading major change, wise leaders pay attention to the sacrifices their followers make. Avoid assumptions about those sacrifices and what constitutes a sacrifice. Recognize genuine sacrifices, tell those stories, and give God glory for being worthy of those costly choices.

Sacrifice Is Proportional

Capital fundraisers have often used the theme, "Not equal gifts, but equal sacrifice" to challenge people to donate financially to major ministry projects. This theme echoes the biblical pattern of proportional giving. Jesus underscored the importance of evaluating gifts proportionally by affirming the woman who gave two small coins (Luke 21:1–4). She was honored because of the ratio of her gift to her resources, not because of the size of her contribution.

Sacrifice is proportional. What constitutes a sacrifice for one person may be pocket change for another. Sorting this out can be complicated when it relates to money, and even more complicated in other areas.

Sacrifice involves proportional self-limiting choices with commodities like money, time, relationships, and rights. Considering all these venues for sacrifice helps create a more holistic view of the subject. Pay attention to the choices followers are making in multiple areas—not just financially—when recognizing their sacrificial efforts to accomplish major ministry changes.

Focus Everything on God's Mission

One final way to glorify God through major change is to keep the ultimate outcome—fulfillment of God's mission—at the forefront throughout the project. Moving a church in Missouri and building a church campus in Oregon were not about getting more visible locations in better neighborhoods. Both projects were about creating more space for families to hear the gospel, respond in faith, and participate in transformational discipleship opportunities. Adopting a new paradigm for a state convention was not about operational efficiency or generational appeal. It was about creating better pathways for churches to work together to share the gospel, meet human needs, start more churches, and train leaders for various ministry venues.

When it came to moving the seminary, the dream was not driven by better facilities in new locations. No one would have sacrificed as much as they did for such a pedestrian purpose. Our vision was thousands more graduates reaching millions more people with the gospel around the world. Relocating the seminary was never the ultimate objective. Our mission is shaping leaders who expand God's kingdom around the world. What we accomplished only had ultimate meaning when directly related to advancing God's kingdom.

God's glory—achieved through advancing his kingdom—must be the ultimate end of every major change. Do not get bogged down or sidetracked by lesser motives. They will frustrate your leadership and demotivate your followers. Focus on the ultimate objective—people transformed into a diverse, global community for God's eternal companionship. With that end in view, major change becomes a joyful, obedient step in the right direction on the adventure of doing ministry in the twenty-first century.

To God be the glory!

Appendices

The following appendices are original documents. They have not been edited or improved for publication—even in hindsight as the projects they launched were implemented and the original plans were changed. These documents, in this form, illustrate using strategic documents and significant presentations, but also show how organizations must adapt as plans resulting from these documents are implemented.

For these reasons, it must be noted that *not everything in these documents proved to be true, was accomplished precisely as described, or came to fruition in the ways first announced.* These appendices are models of what happened in the moment, not what we wish had happened or later happened as the plans were implemented.

Property Sale Agreement Presentation

Dr. Jeff Iorg, President
April 1, 2014

T hank you for gathering today for this important meeting about the future of Golden Gate Seminary. Because I want to be thorough and clear, I will be presenting today from a manuscript. The presentation will take about forty-five minutes. At the conclusion, you will have the opportunity to ask questions in small groups—and later with me directly. You will also receive printed materials and access to electronic materials.

As you know, for the past four years, we have been involved in a lengthy and difficult process related to land development of the Northern California Campus. Let me overview a brief history of that process, where we are today, what will happen in the near future, and then outline some future implications for these decisions.

A Brief History

The master site plan for our property, adopted in 1984, expired at the end of 2009. We knew this was going to happen and took steps to propose a new site plan. This action was required to preserve our entitlements to use the property in the future. This is important to note because some of you have asked why we continue this process when it's so contentious. We have continued it because failure to do so would mean the loss of our rights to build or develop the property in the future—a loss of millions of dollars in property value.

The prolonged political and legal conflict, along with the persistent opposition from some in our community to changing the 1984 plan, has caused us to reconsider all options for the future. We have engaged top planning firms, real estate specialists, financial analysts, legal counsel, and political consultants to help us with this process. Despite these skilled professionals—and much prayer—we have been stymied. We have spent four years and over $1 million so far—with no real progress toward a new master site plan.

For the past four years, our focus has been on developing the Mill Valley Campus property to facilitate fulfillment of our mission and vision. Accomplishing this goal would enable us to continue in this location, but only with incremental improvement of our current model. While future options exist to continue this process, we have little confidence the results will be in our long-term best interest. If we stay on our current path, we are facing years of continued turmoil and uncertainty—and ultimately, a financial crisis.

While we don't often talk about our internal challenges in public, today I need to be frank about our situation. Our Mill Valley campus was designed for a different educational era and a different set of student expectations. Our student housing needs to be replaced. Our academic buildings are outdated and need to be rebuilt. Our infrastructure— things like plumbing, electrical, and mechanical systems—are invisible problems which will cost millions to replace. These are all serious problems snowballing toward us.

Our economic model and the price points set by our need to be comparably priced to other Southern Baptist seminaries makes meeting these financial demands very difficult. We would need to triple tuition and double housing rental rates to be able to maintain our campus in the economic climate of Marin County. Those kinds of changes are simply not possible. Our generous donors are financially astute. They have been unwilling to make significant gifts toward facility improvements, asking instead why we continue to try to operate in such an expensive location.

Sometimes, God allows obstacles like these to teach us perseverance. Other times, he erects barriers to redirect us. For the past four years, we have interpreted the challenges we have faced as obstacles to overcome. Over the past year, however, we have gradually changed our perspective and believe these obstacles are signposts telling us to go another direction.

A Defined Mission

Over the past few months, our executive leaders and Board of Trustees have refocused on how the current situation relates to fulfilling our mission statement adopted in 2009.

Our mission is clear: Shaping leaders who expand God's kingdom around the world. Our mission is not land development. It's not campus preservation. It's not fighting legal battles. It's not preserving institutional legacy. Our mission is shaping leaders. Whatever we do in the future must be driven by our mission.

A Clearly Articulated Vision

A new perspective must also be guided by our vision statement. Golden Gate articulated its vision in a fresh statement in 2009:

We will be a world-class seminary with an international reputation for biblical scholarship while advocating innovative, effective ministry methods. We will focus on urban mission strategies while maintaining our contextual commitment to train leaders for churches in all settings in the Western United States.

We will operate multiple campuses and learning centers, as well as an extensive electronic delivery system providing a high quality educational experience. Our faculty will be well-known, both as scholars and models of ministerial effectiveness. Our staff will be competent models of servant leadership. Our students will be in high demand as global leaders in all aspects of kingdom work.

We will be financially sound, accruing significant endowment through strategic resource management and donor development. We will emphasize affordability for students, enabling graduates to deploy unencumbered by significant seminary debt.

We will pursue our mission with passion, living out the Great Commission and the Great Commandment by the grace of our Lord Jesus Christ.

These are more than words on paper. These words motivate me every day as I make decisions about the seminary. The decisions we are announcing today are driven by our best understanding of how to fulfill our mission and vision in the future.

A New Direction for the Future

The question before us then, is this: "What land development option best fulfills our mission and vision in the twenty-first century?" As I said earlier, sometimes, God allows obstacles to teach us perseverance. Other times, he erects barriers to change our direction. I now believe God is using current barriers to direct us down a new path toward a new answer to this key question.

The first definitive step forward in this journey has been taken. I am announcing today Golden Gate Seminary has signed an agreement to sell all seminary-owned property in Marin County to North Coast Land Holdings.

The sale agreement has been unanimously approved by the Board of Trustees. We are now in a period of due diligence with a goal of closing the sale later this summer. At that point, the terms of the final sale can be disclosed. Like most real estate transactions, the period of due diligence is a time of investigation and continued negotiation. For that reason, we need to wait until everything is concluded before prematurely announcing the final terms of sale.

What does this mean for the immediate future?

This is dramatic, even shocking news, for many of you. Your immediate natural reaction is probably, "What does this mean for me?" Let me begin answering that question by summarizing some key aspects of this decision for the immediate future.

First, we are now in a time of uncertainty regarding the status of our property. While we have tried to minimize the length of time for the due diligence process, a reasonable time frame for public consideration and county action is a required part of a legal transaction like this one. I know this is unsettling for all of us, but it is a normal part of a major land sale. I am counting on you, as the saying goes, "to keep calm and carry on" until these issues are resolved.

Second, if the sale is finalized, we will continue to operate the Mill Valley campus for two more academic years just as we do today. We have arranged to lease the property for our continued use through 2016. This means the seminary will be in this location, fully operational, for the rest of this academic year, plus two additional academic years. It is imperative we communicate clearly the seminary is open for business and fully operational during this transition.

Third, when the sale is finalized, our academic programs and administrative functions will remain the same in the immediate future. For the next two years, we will be fully operational in our current locations. You will come to work, teach your classes, and do the things you are doing now to keep the seminary strong.

What does this mean for the long-term future?

Another important question is, "What does the mean for the long-term future?" Let me also summarize key aspects of this decision for the long-term future.

Campus Locations

After the sale is finalized, we will make major changes to our future campus operations. We will relocate our primary campus to a new campus in Southern California and open a new Bay Area regional campus in a more commuter-friendly location.

Both church and population demographic projections for the next forty years call for the primary campus to serve the Western United States to be in Southern California. Our new primary campus will be intentionally located in the fastest growing population center in the West, in a multicultural context, symbolizing the seminary's commitment to taking the gospel to every kind of community. The new campus will be modern, flexible, and cost-efficient. It will look very different than a traditional seminary campus. We will capitalize on this choice, not apologize for it. We will highlight the contrast with other campus-intensive seminaries, not minimize it. Making this choice will enable us to invest money in people and programs, not maintenance and facilities.

Our new primary campus will include academic, administrative, library, worship, and student gathering space. It will become the new administrative hub for our regional campuses, online programs, future teaching sites, and national and international training centers.

As part of expanding this system, the seminary will also open a new Bay Area regional campus, to support Bay Area commuter students. This new Bay Area regional campus will open in August 2016.

One way to look at this change is this: We are reversing the roles of our California campuses. The primary campus will be at a new location in Southern California with a new regional campus in the Bay Area.

Impact on Students

After the sale is finalized, we will maintain the academic programs and standards currently in place across our system. We will continue to offer degrees through both face-to-face and online instruction, as well as continue hybrid programs at regional campuses across the west. CLD will continue in its current format.

Current residential students at the Mill Valley Campus will have the balance of this academic year, plus two more full years to complete their degree programs at the current location. We will work with every student who cannot finish on that timetable to assure they can complete their program as seamlessly as possible. All other students (Northern California commuters, regional students, online students, non-residential doctoral students, and CLD students) should experience no disruption in their academic programs.

Impact on Employees

After the sale is finalized, here are some of the challenges and changes employees can anticipate. Current employees will experience some disruption as a normal outcome of major organizational change. While we will work to minimize negative impact, it would be unreasonable to expect to avoid it completely.

In the future, some current NCC and SCC employees will relocate to the new primary campus in Southern California; some current NCC employees will continue to live in the Bay Area and teach at both future California campuses; some employees may resign; some will end their service through graduation or spousal graduation; some will retire; and some will be terminated when this campus closes.

Decisions about individual employees will be made as soon as possible. Some of these decisions will need to wait until the new primary campus and Bay Area regional campus locations are found and final staffing plans are determined. We expect to announce those decisions by early 2015—meaning employees will then have about eighteen months to adjust to new employment options.

Additional Strategic Changes

After the sale is finalized, there are several other strategic changes that will be implemented. We can't announce these until the sale is finalized. Changing our locations is the most visible change, but there are others that will also be very significant. We will be making major changes in our technological capabilities, web presence, marketing and recruiting strategies, staffing structures, housing policies, and seminary identity.

We have identified about one hundred action items that will require our attention—but most of these can't be addressed until the sale process is finalized. To do so would be premature and distract us from the important work we need to do in the next few months. We aren't avoiding these issues today, just saying it's not yet time to engage these future issues.

So, while these changes announced today are significant, you can expect the next few years to be a time of continued change as we move toward the future together. I know this is unsettling. You want decisions to be more definite and to happen quickly. This kind of organizational change takes time and patience. Some of us have been living with this uncertainty for four years. We know how unsettling it is and will give you all the information we can, as soon as we can, as we move forward together.

What Happens Next?

As we near the end of this presentation, let me pose one final question, "What happens next?"

First, you will have an opportunity to ask questions and begin to process this information. We are going to do this by groups. The faculty will meet with Mike Martin. Students will meet with Adam Groza.

Staff employees will meet with Gary Groat. I will take questions from regional campus employees over the phone. I will also be in my conference room from 3:00–4:00 for anyone who wants to ask me questions or talk with me directly.

Second, this information is being released through all media today. This news is being released by video on our website, on Baptist Press, by email to 6,000 addresses in our database, by mail to 12,000 addresses, and through social media.

Third, you will soon start receiving questions about these decisions. Answer them as best you can. Don't speculate or say more than you know. This is very important. We know how fast rumors can spread on social media. Help us by spreading only the facts, without speculation or embellishment. Refer people to your vice president or to me if you don't know the answer to a question you are asked. We have also prepared a list of frequently asked questions that will be on the website to help you provide solid answers. You will also have a copy of this presentation as a resource for answering future questions.

Fourth, come to work tomorrow and do your job. Come to class tomorrow and continue to study. The seminary is fully operational. We are working on a possible relocation of services, not a closure. We are open for business in every way.

Conclusion

Now let me conclude with some personal words.

These next few months are a time of real risk for us. We have signed a Sale Agreement but we have not closed the sale. I wish there were some other way to do this process, which would have kept us from this uncertainty. But, to use a worn out expression, "it is what it is" and we will go through it together—riding a roller coaster of emotions—but eventually coming through to either a "sale" or a "no sale" conclusion. While the outcome is uncertain, there is a very high probability we will close the sale later this summer.

I know your individual responses at this point are many and varied. Some of you may be too shocked to respond at all. Some may be angry—feeling like we have sold out rather than stayed here at all cost. Some may be disappointed because of your profound attachment to this location. Some of you may be confused and just want to ask a lot questions. I understand your responses will vary. I'm ready to receive whatever you need to ask or say.

On the other hand, some of you are already dreaming about future possibilities. You can't wait to get on with the adventure. You realize this is a historic day in American Christianity. You are part of a seminary that is willing to risk everything to pursue its mission.

We are walking away from a beautiful location, but we are not walking away from our mission. We are leaving behind a dilapidated campus, resource-draining political and legal turmoil, and financial demands which are getting more and more difficult to manage. But this decision is not about what we are leaving behind. It's about the future we are headed toward.

Today, you are part of one of the boldest moves by any seminary in the past century. We are selling a campus, not closing our doors. We are relocating and repositioning for future success, not abandoning our vision. We are sacrificing short-term comfort for long-term fulfillment of our mission. We are positioning ourselves strategically, geographically, and financially to impact the Western United States and the world like never before.

We will all pay a personal cost for fulfilling our mission and vision this way. It will, at times, be scary and unnerving. Nevertheless, as I have told you on countless occasions, "The mission matters most." Like perhaps no seminary in recent history, we are standing behind that declaration with our actions today.

In my heart of hearts, I believe these decisions are right. I have agonized over them, and have come to believe this is God's path for us. I am going forward, with every intention of finalizing the sale agreement and building a new kind of seminary for the twenty-first century.

I have made these decisions with many regrets but ultimately, no doubts. We are headed to the future and I hope you will join me on the journey.

A Fresh Statement

About the future by the churches and people of the Northwest Baptist Convention

Our Identity

We are a regional network of churches working together to fulfill the Great Commission of Jesus Christ.

Our Vision

We will do whatever it takes to effectively share the good news of Jesus Christ throughout the cultures of the Northwest and build strong churches that will impact their communities and the world.

Our Objectives

We work together, believing churches can do more through cooperation than by individual effort, to accomplish these shared objectives:
▸ Develop and encourage ministry leaders
▸ Promote evangelism and balanced church growth
▸ Facilitate starting new churches and mission ministries
▸ Provide a channel for worldwide missions involvement

Our Strategy

We rely on churches and associations to initiate field-based strategies to fulfill our vision and employ our convention staff to assist them according to our shared objectives.

Appendix 3

Greater Gresham Baptist Church

Mission Statement

Our mission is to tell the good news of Jesus Christ to all people everywhere and guide those who believe to full maturity in Him.

Vision Statement

We envision a church that designs its ministries to appeal to and meet the needs of non-Christians. Because of this the church has some innovative methods, schedules, and programs, and experiences continual and consistent growth. After a period of slower growth at the beginning while a strong foundation is being laid, our church begins to reach more and more people. After a few years, several hundred people are gathering each week for dynamic worship in multiple services.

During this time the church is also working to build a comprehensive ministry program which not only reaches people but guides them as they grow in their relationship to Christ. With a strong emphasis on strengthening families, the church develops ministries to men, women, teenagers, children, and preschoolers. The church becomes known for its professional pastoral staff and its strong leadership team.

As part of its growth, the church becomes directly involved in missions by sponsoring new churches in the Northwest and by sending ministry teams to foreign countries. It also becomes an encouragement to other churches and a catalyst for growth among churches of all denominations in the Northwest.

Values—Statements

1. We value simplicity over complexity.
2. We value flexibility over rigidity.
3. We value balance over imbalance.
4. We value effectiveness over efficiency.
5. We value risk and failure over the status quo.

A Seminary for the Twenty-First Century

A Presentation to the Seminary Community
Dr. Jeff Iorg, President
August 2014

T hank you for gathering today to hear some important information about our future ministry. This presentation will be done in two parts. First, I will address issues related to property and relocation. Second, I will then address a variety of issues related to the transition. These presentations are quite detailed and will take about two hours. I am making the first part of this presentation from a manuscript to help me stay on track and systematize the information. You will have an opportunity to ask questions later in the meeting. After the meeting, you will have access to printed, electronic, and video resources containing this information.

On April 1, 2014, I announced the pending sale of our property near Mill Valley, California. That sale is now complete. We are now leasing back our former property and will continue to operate on that site until June 2016. Thank you for your patience during this unsettling transition time. You have done a remarkable job maintaining your focus on doing your job and fulfilling our mission. Thank you for rising to the occasion and modeling the best of Christian grace and service. In just a few days, hundreds of students will fill our actual and virtual classrooms. I am proud of all of you and the work you are doing to continue to train those students for future kingdom service.

Golden Gate now has a remarkable opportunity to chart a new course as a seminary for the twenty-first century. The property sale was the first step. Today's presentation will provide many more details about how we will move forward.

While the most visible aspects of this opportunity are locations and facilities, the circumstances leading to this change have occasioned—even mandated—we reconsider core issues related to the methods and approaches for accomplishing the seminary's mission.

Let me make two broad observations at the outset of this report. First, while changing locations is difficult—replacing long-held paradigms, changing operational patterns, and establishing a fresh identity will be even more difficult. It will require our best effort to truly become a seminary for the twenty-first century. Second, while making these changes will be difficult, we must respond to the realities of seminary-life today. We must acknowledge the seminary we are (not the seminary we imagine ourselves to be), the seminary we are becoming (based on the realities of student demographics), and the seminary that must emerge (so we will viable for the long-term future).

We must, in short, seize the opportunity and become a new seminary for the twenty-first century.

Will It Really Be a *New* Seminary?

A legitimate question is, "Will it really be a new seminary?" Because so many things about our future will be different, the answer is yes. But there are clearly some unchanging aspects of the seminary that will be carried forward as a strong foundation for the future.

These include:

1.   Confessional doctrinal integrity and denominational affiliation.

2. High academic standards and full accreditation of academic programs.

3. Financial strength including endowments, lack of debt, and reputation for integrity.

4. Online campus, regional campuses, and a national certificate-level training program.

5. Faculty and staff who serve with passion and distinction.

6. Presence in the American West and partnerships with western state conventions.

7. Donors, alumni, and friends who stand with us as we move ahead.

There are also significant changes, however, that will be part of the new seminary and merit calling it a new seminary—or at least a new *kind of* seminary—for the twenty-first century:

1. New focus on our mission and vision—We are creating greater alignment with our core mission and vision through the process of making strategic decisions about the seminary's future.

2. New perspective on facilities—We will function with more efficient, more flexible, and more technologically advanced facilities with fewer restrictions on future use.

3. New identity—We are naturally evolving because of a new primary campus location, our continued regionalization in the American West, our emerging ability to teach globally, and the changing nature of our public perception.

4. New focus on directing resources to our mission—We will use fewer resources on land development, deferred maintenance, property management, future building needs, and future building choices.

5. New commitment to contemporary educational methods—We will embrace online delivery, video classrooms, webcasting,

digital libraries, and other information storage and delivery methods.

6. New programs—We will change to meet the needs of and take advantage of the strengths of the churches in a new primary location.

7. New faculty and staff—We will experience inevitable change resulting from new people who become part of our team.

While there are many aspects of the seminary that will be carried forward, there are enough strategic changes to posit the results as producing a new seminary for the twenty-first century. The following sections of this report provide some additional details about the first three of these areas of newness and change—a new focus on mission and vision, new facilities, and a new identity.

A New Focus on Mission and Vision

A Defined Mission

As we considered the options related to potential relocation, we turned to our mission statement for guidance on the final decision. Our mission is clear: "Shaping leaders who expand God's kingdom around the world." We determined our mission was not land development. It was not campus preservation or maintaining institutional legacy. It was not winning legal battles or defining our destiny by a particular location. Our mission is shaping leaders who preach the gospel, evangelize the lost, disciple the converted, congregationalize believers, and lead others to do the same.

We are currently making important decisions based on fulfilling our mission. We are attempting, in fresh ways, to bring greater congruity to all aspects of seminary life—from campus locations to housing policies to enrollment strategies to academic programs—based on our mission. While there are always inconsistencies in every organization and misguided choices by every leader, we are striving for greater decisional alignment so that all aspects of who we are serve our mission more effectively.

A Clearly Articulated Vision

We are also making significant strides toward fulfilling our vision. We articulated our vision in a compelling, fresh statement in 2009:

> We will be a world-class seminary with an international reputation for biblical scholarship while advocating innovative, effective ministry methods. We will focus on urban mission strategies while maintaining our contextual commitment to train leaders for churches in all settings in the Western United States.
>
> We will operate multiple campuses and learning centers, as well as an extensive electronic delivery system providing a high quality educational experience. Our faculty will be well-known, both as scholars and models of ministerial effectiveness. Our staff will be competent models of servant leadership. Our students will be in high demand as global leaders in all aspects of kingdom work.
>
> We will be financially sound, accruing significant endowment through strategic resource management and donor development. We will emphasize affordability for students, enabling graduates to deploy unencumbered by significant seminary debt.
>
> We will pursue our mission with passion, living out the Great Commission and the Great Commandment by the grace of our Lord Jesus Christ."

Our mission and vision are clear. Fulfilling them is and will be a continuing challenge. We have renewed our focus on mission-discipline and vision-fulfillment—which mandate changes resulting in a new seminary for the twenty-first century.

A New Perspective on Facilities

Core Functions for the New Primary Campus

The relocation raises the question of the kind of new primary campus facilities needed to fulfill our mission and vision. In essence, three things are required to accomplish our mission—a student, a teacher, and a means for them to communicate. A leader can be shaped by conversing with a teacher under a shade tree—student, teacher, means. That's the essence of our work, but what happens as growth occurs?

When additional students gather, a class results. When more teachers gather, a faculty results. When even more "teachers" gather, a library results. Convenience and efficiency call for buildings to house those functions. We worship as part of our training, so chapel space is helpful. When all of this happens in one place with a large enough number of people, administrative support space is also needed. The end result is a physical campus.

This description of the essence of fulfilling our mission, while overly simplified, is still helpful. The core facilities a seminary needs are space for students, faculty, library, worship, and administration. This means our campus in the future needs classrooms, student gathering space, faculty offices, a library, a chapel, and administrative space.

What about other buildings like gyms, swimming pools, exercise rooms, child care centers, bookstores, dining halls, maintenance buildings, and other similar facilities? While there is nothing wrong with having them, they are not necessary for accomplishing our mission. They may be helpful, but they are not essential. While other schools may have them, building them just to "keep up with the Joneses" is not a strategically acceptable reason.

Besides the "functional question," we must also ask the "stewardship question" about using money on these kinds of facilities. All of these facilities require significant resources to build and maintain. If they are not essential for our mission, even if we have the money or could raise the money to provide them, should we build them? For me, the answer is "no." There are simply too many other pressing financial needs in the kingdom to devote resources to lesser items.

When millions of people have not yet even heard the name of Jesus, our school must model frugality and simplicity to prioritize resources for global missions. Our tuition must be kept low so students can graduate without seminary-created debt. Our future resources must be focused on people and programs—not facilities. Our national convention has called on every church, association, and state convention to economize and spend more money on direct mission activity. We have an opportunity to model doing this as a national entity and we must seize the moment to fulfill this mandate.

Key Factors for Selecting a New Primary Campus

Besides considering the core functions and stewardship issues about new buildings, there were ten determining factors we identified as significant in selecting the future primary campus site. These were previously communicated in Transition Update 4 sent to the seminary community in April 2014. Let me summarize them again.

One: Timetable

The new site must be finished and occupied by July 1, 2016.

Two: Size

The new site must provide at least 100-125,000 square feet of usable building space for classrooms, offices, library, chapel, and administrative functions.

Three: Rental Housing

The new site must have a wide-range of rental housing available within a 20 minute drive from the campus—from economy housing for students to nicer rental property for employees.

Four: Housing for Purchase

The new site must have a wide-range of housing available for purchase within a 20 minute drive from the campus—from lower price townhomes to nicer single family homes.

Five: Commuter Housing

The new site must have access to commuter housing—for doctoral students, commuting students, potential new students, and other commuter-housing users.

Six: Parking

The new site must have adequate parking to meet local building codes.

Seven: Transportation Accessibility

The new site must be easily accessible by existing transportation systems. It must be located close to major freeways and a major airport. It would also be advantageous to be on public transportation routes.

Eight: Impressive Presence

The new site must be impressive. While we must avoid opulence creating the impression of wasted resources, the new site must be an elegant, high-quality statement of our identity. It must be in a developing area that will hold its value for the next thirty years. The site should have solid resale value to allow future flexibility for the seminary.

Nine: Located in the Inland Empire

Both church and population demographics indicate this is the most missional location for a seminary serving primarily in the Western United States for the next thirty years.

Ten: Budget

The new site must be made fully operational within the budget the Board has set for relocation. While the sale of our property has produced significant resources for the future, funds are still limited and we must use the money wisely.

Finding New Facilities

After we identified the core functions, stewardship issues, and ten key site selection factors, the challenge was finding facilities that met as many of the criteria as possible. Over the past few years, we have monitored property options in Southern California. In December 2013, when it appeared the sale of the Mill Valley property was likely, we intensified our efforts at discovering campus site options. We toured several sites and analyzed options should the sale actually happen.

In April 2014, just after announcing the sale agreement for the Mill Valley property, we formally engaged a real estate broker in Southern California. He provided a detailed analysis of property options in a large triangle from Pomona to Temecula to Redlands and also in eastern Orange County. We considered about forty properties of all types—raw land, ready-to-build land, and existing buildings.

Ultimately, we selected a primary site and initiated negotiations about a possible purchase. The Board of Trustees then voted unanimously to pursue this primary site. We have now signed a purchase and sale agreement for this property and are in the process of finalizing plans so we can obtain a Conditional Use Permit. Let me introduce you to the new facility.

The New Primary Campus

The new primary campus is a six-story commercial building, adjacent ready-to-build lot, and parking lot in Ontario, California. The building was constructed in 2009 and has remained vacant, due to the economic downturn, since that time. It has never been occupied.

The building is a "warm shell"—meaning it is finished on the exterior, has all mechanical systems installed throughout, but has an unfinished interior. The adjacent buildable lot is already entitled for a future building. The purchase also includes all the parking entitlements assigned to both the existing building and the vacant lot.

Here is a summary of the property when analyzed by the ten factors listed above.

One: Timetable

The site can be purchased, finished, and in use prior to July 1, 2016. We have employed TR Design as our architects. They are an award winning campus design firm. As an added bonus, they are believers who understand and share our mission. We are on schedule to submit our request for a Conditional Use Permit by October 1, 2014, begin construction in early 2015, and move in by early 2016.

Two: Size

The building is approximately 153,000 gross square feet. The adjacent lot is entitled to build an additional 75,000 square feet of space which can be used for a chapel, library, offices, class-rooms, etc. (Up to 150,000 square feet could be built with the addition of a parking garage.) As a comparison, the gross square footage of our current primary campus core buildings (admin-istration, academic, library, and cafeteria) is approximately 121,000. The new building is about 20 percent larger than our current facilities with room to expand to almost double the size of our current buildings.

Three: Rental housing

The site has hundreds of apartments with a variety of rental pricing within a 20 minute drive.

Four: Housing for purchase

The site has thousands of homes and townhomes, priced from $300,000, within a 20 minute drive. This includes several planned communities about 6 minutes from the site and a new planned community of several hundred homes about 12 minutes from the site.

Five: Commuter housing

The site has a discount hotel across the street that will be contracted for commuter housing.

Six: Parking

The site includes 711 parking spaces as the parking entitlements associated with the building and the vacant lot. This exceeds code requirements for our proposed use.

Seven: Transportation accessibility

The site is two blocks from the 10 freeway, about a mile from both the 15 and 60 freeways, and across the street from the Ontario Airport.

Eight: Impressive presence

The site is in an upscale office park, near five for-profit universities, in an area that is still developing, and will retain its value for many years. The existing building is Class A office space, with high-quality exterior finishes, mature landscaping, and facing a small lake.

Nine: Located in the Inland Empire

The site is in a major transportation and shopping hub for the area—across the street from the Ontario Airport, near Ontario Mills Mall, Citizens Bank Arena, Ontario Convention Center, hotels, restaurants, and other attractions.

Ten: Budget

We have negotiated a purchase price of $26 million for the building, adjoining lot, landscaped parking, and all approved entitlements. Finishing the building will cost $8-9 million. This totals $35 million.

The cost breakdown might be understood this way—the base price for the building is about $144 per square foot and the cost of the adjacent lot is about $4 million. The finished cost for the building will be about $210 per square foot. The replacement cost for this building today is $300 per square foot.

The Board has allocated $35 million from the sale proceeds, plus endowment earnings and other earnings for the relocation. The Board has reserved the balance of the sale proceeds, $50 million, for our endowment.

A New Seminary Identity

An oft-asked question related to our relocation has been "Is the seminary going to change its name?" The name Golden Gate Seminary connects us with a beautiful bridge and rich heritage in the San Francisco Bay Area. Under that name, we have sent more than 8,000 graduates across America and around the world. We celebrate our alumni and value our history. Our current name has served us well and helped define our identity.

The possibility of a name change is a controversial and problematic aspect of the relocation for some. They fear changing our name may result in diminishing our historical identity, alienating our alumni, or undergoing other risks associated with such a change. Those concerns certainly must be, and have been, considered.

Another interesting factor is our Board of Trustees cannot change our name. It can only be done by the Southern Baptist Convention, voting in session at two consecutive summer meetings. Any name change will be a slow process.

We have a growing sense; however, that bearing a name so closely associated with an iconic landmark won't serve us as well when our primary campus is in the Inland Empire east of Los Angeles. Ever since we have been seriously considering relocating, we have also been analyzing the options and factors related to a new name. While there are many challenges with making such a change, choosing to do so now—while we are relocating—is the wisest course of action.

We will soon initiate specific steps in that direction with the SBC Executive Committee, and ultimately the Southern Baptist Convention.

A New Name

The seminary will establish a new identity by asking the SBC to change our legal name to—*Gateway Seminary of the Southern Baptist Convention*. The primary designator "Gateway Seminary" will be used in public communication. This name is desirable for several reasons:

1. It eliminates geographic identity—since our program can be offered anywhere in the world.
2. It differentiates us from other SBC seminaries by breaking the denominational pattern of geographic names.
3. It gives us the opportunity to build a new evangelical brand—managing the message of how we market ourselves to accentuate our strengths.
4. It connects to our heritage as Golden Gate Seminary—Gateway is already the name of our magazine.
5. It connects with a biblical motif—Jesus is the Gate (John 10:7, 9).
6. It has multiple marketing angles—gateway to your future, gateway to the world, gateway to your ministry, etc.
7. It is distinctive—no other seminary has this name.
8. It retains our Baptist identity and denominational affiliation.
9. It can be used with our award winning logo, nameplate, and tag line.

10. It follows the well-received pattern established by LifeWay Christian Resources of the SBC and Guidestone Financial Resources of the SBC.

A Slow Process

Any name change must be adopted two consecutive years by the Southern Baptist Convention. The seminary will take appropriate steps to work through this process with the SBC Executive Committee. The new name will likely be voted on the first time in June 2015 and, if approved by the SBC, become official in June 2016 (the same month we relocate).

We are taking the necessary legal steps toward adopting this new name. We are making sure we can carry forward our assets, receive future bequests, and develop an appropriate online identity. We will also communicate to our alumni and constituents what this will mean for them. We will continue to operate—in every way—as Golden Gate Seminary until the official vote by the SBC in June 2016.

Conclusion

As we come to the end of this presentation, let's revisit what I said on April 1, 2014 when I announced the land sale and relocation. I said:

> "We are walking away from a beautiful location, but we are not walking away from our mission. We are leaving behind a dilapidated campus, resource-draining political and legal turmoil, and financial demands which are getting more and more difficult to manage. But this decision is not about what we are leaving behind. It's about the future we are headed toward."

Today, you have learned more specifically what this means for us. We are moving toward a beautiful new facility designed for a new paradigm of seminary education and establishing a new identity that will define a global educational delivery institution. Our future is becoming clearer, and I hope more exciting to you. In my previous presentation, I added:

> "You are part of one of the boldest moves by any seminary in the past century. We are selling a campus, not closing our doors. We are relocating and repositioning for future success, not abandoning our vision. We are sacrificing short-term comfort for long-term fulfillment of our mission. We are positioning ourselves strategically, geographically, and financially to impact the Western United States and the world like never before."

Today, you can see more fully how we are positioning ourselves. We are stronger today than we have ever been—spiritually, academically, strategically, and financially. Our transition has been and will be costly—but the resulting seminary will be worth it now and for the generations that come after us. I concluded the previous speech by saying:

> "We will all pay a personal cost for fulfilling our mission and vision this way. It will, at times, be scary and unnerving. Nevertheless, as I have told you on countless occasions, 'The mission matters most.' Like perhaps no seminary in recent history, we are standing behind that declaration with our actions today. In my heart of hearts, I believe these decisions are right. I have agonized over them, and have come to believe this is God's path for us. I am going forward, with every intention of finalizing the sale agreement and building a new kind of seminary for the twenty-first century. I have made these decisions with many regrets but ultimately, no doubts. We are headed to the future and I hope you will join me on the journey."

I have not wavered on my conclusion. We are headed to the future—a much more defined future than I was able to tell you about in April. You have joined me on the journey with a much more positive response than was expected or deserved. Thank you for standing together so far. I am counting on you to complete the task of creating Gateway Seminary—a seminary for the twenty-first century.

Some people outside our seminary family have told me they marvel at our unity, focus, and determination. People are amazed we are facing unprecedented change without division and rancor. We are trying to do what has never been done before—move one of the largest seminaries in the world 400 miles and redefine our identity for a new century, all while remaining fully operational. It is a daunting, seemingly impossible task. A few weeks ago, Dr. Durst sent me this slide:

"The person who says something is impossible should not interrupt the person who is doing it."

You are doing the impossible. Fifty years from now, employees will tell the story of the amazing people who propelled the seminary into the future they are enjoying. You are part of that story and I am proud to be part of it with you. Let's print, paint, draw, or needlepoint this slide and put it up in our workspace to remind us what we are doing every day. While others say it can't be done, you are doing the impossible. You are building a seminary for the twenty-first century.

Let's conclude the first part of our meeting with your questions about what I have covered so far. Then, I will share some additional information about other transition issues.

Notes

1. Joseph C. Rost, *Leadership for the Twenty-First Century* (Westport, CT: Praeger, 1993), 41.

2. Dictionary.com, s.v., "Leadership," accessed December 19, 2016, http://www.dictionary.com/browse/leadership.

3. Rost, *Leadership for the Twenty-First Century*, 69–88.

4. Camel: a racehorse designed by a committee.

5. Rost, *Leadership for the Twenty-First Century*, 91.

6. Ibid., 102.

7. Everett M. Rogers, *Diffusion of Innovations* (New York: Free Press, 1962).

8. John P. Kotter, *Leading Change* (Boston: Harvard Business School Press, 1996).

9. John P. Kotter, *A Sense of Urgency* (Boston: Harvard Business Press, 2008).

10. Calvin Miller, *The Empowered Leader: 10 Keys to Servant Leadership* (Nashville: Broadman & Holman, 1995), 82

11. William Bridges, *Managing Transitions: Making the Most of Change* (Philadelphia: Da Capo, 2009), 3.

12. Jeff Iorg, *The Character of Leadership: Nine Qualities that Define Great Leaders* (Nashville: B&H, 2007), 47–69.

13. See Elisabeth Kulber-Ross and David Kessler, *On Grief and Dying: Finding the Meaning of Grief Through the Five Stages of Loss* (New York: Scribner, 2005); H. Norman Wright, *Experiencing Grief* (Nashville: B&H, 2004).

14. Jeff Iorg, *The Case for Antioch: A Biblical Model for a Transformational Church* (Nashville, TN: B&H, 2011), 38–46.

15. Jeff Iorg, *Seasons of a Leader's Life: Learning, Leading, and Leaving your Legacy* (Nashville, TN: B&H, 2013).

16. Jeff Iorg, *Uncommon Courage* (Birmingham, AL: New Hope Publishers, 2017).

17. Westminster Assembly, Douglas F. Kelly, Phillip R. Rollinson, and Frederisk T. Marsh, *The Westminster Shorter Catechism in Modern English* (Philipsburg, NJ: Presbyterian and Reformed, 1986).